THE NEW TESTAMENT

J. CHRISTIAAN BEKER

THE NEW TESTAMENT
A Thematic Introduction

FORTRESS PRESS   Minneapolis

To all my students whose commitment to the ministry has taught me over the years the true meaning of biblical scholarship.

THE NEW TESTAMENT
A Thematic Introduction

Scripture quotations, unless otherwise noted, are from the New Revised Standard Version of the Bible, copyright © 1989 by the Division of Christian Education of the National Council of the Churches of Christ in the United States of America.

Library of Congress Cataloging-in-Publication Data

Beker, Johan Christiaan, 1924–
    The New Testament : a thematic introduction / J. Christiaan Beker.
      p.   cm.
    Includes bibliographical references.
    ISBN 0-8006-2775-X :
    1. Bible. N.T.—Introductions.   2. Bible. N.T.—Theology.
I. Title.
BS2330.2.B45   1994
225.6'1—dc20   93-32244
                                                   CIP

Manufactured in the U.S.A.   AF 1–2775

98   97   96   95   94   1   2   3   4   5   6   7   8   9   10

CONTENTS

CHAPTER 1

Introduction

FOR MORE THAN TWO DECADES I HAVE TAUGHT A BASIC INTRODUC-tory course of the New Testament to first-year seminary students. During that time, my approach to the subject matter has changed considerably. I decided to move away from a "textbook" format to a more religious-oriented emphasis to allow the historical text of the New Testament to become transparent for today's readers.

I now present these lectures to a wider audience in the hope that the New Testament text may execute its challenge and claim anew for our time. The reader should be aware at the outset of the following restraints and guidelines:

1. Instead of dealing with all twenty-seven books of the New Testament, I have selected what, in my opinion, are the most significant books. Moreover, my selectivity involves not only a choice among the books of the New Testament but also a preference for a limited number of crucial themes and issues within the books themselves.

This procedure aims at clarity and focus. Rather than asking the readers to appropriate an exhaustive and full-blown treatment of every theme in every book of the New Testament, I invite them to concentrate on some of the most central issues within the New Testament. In this way, I hope to counter the possible disappointment of readers in omitting certain sections of the New Testament.

Sixteen of the twenty-seven books of the New Testament are discussed; the only significant omissions are the seven Catholic Epistles, which are represented by 1 Peter.

2. I follow an essentially chronological sequence of the New Testament books in these lectures, so that the letters of Paul precede the discussion of the Gospels. However, two post-Pauline documents are treated in conjunction with Paul's letters in order to demonstrate their similarities and dissimilarities with those of Paul.

3. Although it will be obvious that there is a wide variety and diversity between the New Testament documents in their presentation of the gospel, the issue of their unity will be my concern not only in the final chapter but will occupy me throughout.

4. In conformity with my intention to focus on the claim of the New Testament, I will restrict the investigation of historical, political, and socioeconomic backgrounds of the texts to a minimum, except when their relevance for the understanding of the message of the text requires it.

5. I will adopt an exegetical method that is based on two fundamental principles:

a. The investigation of the relation between the whole and the parts of a paragraph/section of a New Testament text-unit is crucial for its understanding. That is, the context of a specific verse must always be kept in mind, so as to prevent a "prooftexting" of a text thus isolating it from its semantic surroundings.

b. A respect for the normative and canonical claim of the New Testament for all forms of Christian theology is my guide for these lectures. It prompts me to adopt what I call a "catalytic hermeneutic," by which I mean the attempt to state the abiding and normative claim of the New Testament text. Such a "catalytic hermeneutic" will avoid both a timeless treatment of the text and an ideological distortion of it. A timeless treatment assumes that the New Testament text was written for every possible time and worldview, whereas an ideological understanding of the text imposes its own contemporary conviction on the text.

In contrast to those schemes, a "catalytic hermeneutic" pays attention to both the historical specificity of the text and its transparent claim on our world. I call these twin concerns the relation of coherence and contingency. By coherence, I mean the abiding-normative dimension of the text; by contingency, its historical and situational dimension that addresses the particular historical time of the text.

It will become clear that the interrelation between coherence and contingency safeguards the two elements that are essential to the proclamation of the gospel today. For the contingent element of the gospel safeguards its claim to constitute a word on target for the particular needs of its addressees, whereas the coherent element of the gospel protects its normative, abiding quality.

Indeed, it is essential to the gospel that both its authenticity and relevance be secured. There are two dangers that beset the proclamation of the gospel: often we tend to neglect either the coherence of the gospel or its contingency. In the first case, the dialogical character of the gospel — that is, the interaction between coherence and contingency — is sacrificed for the sake of a monological imposition of the coherence of the gospel at the price of neglecting its contingent address, that is, its dogmatic imposition on every possible situation and problem that people face. In the second case, the opposite occurs — the coherence of the gospel is sacrificed for the sake of its presumable relevance. In other words, the pressures of the contingent situation lead to a neglect of the abiding coherent claim of the gospel, so that the only thing that counts is an opportunistic assessment of "what the market today will buy." There can be little doubt that whereas evangelical fundamentalism succumbs to the first danger, liberal theologians often fall prey to the second one.

This volume will center on the relation of authenticity and relevance — that is, on what I call the interaction between coherence and contingency. In using this method, I hope to show the transparency inherent in the historical texts of the New Testament so that they may come to speak in the clarity of our own language.

6. We must be aware that the hermeneutical task — the task of understanding a text — involves three interrelated aspects:

a. *speech*, which brings the obscure into the clarity of linguistic expression;

b. *translation*, which transfers an obscure, foreign language into the clarity of one's own language;

c. *commentary*, which explicates the meaning of obscure language by means of clearer language.[1]

It is clear that all three aspects of the hermeneutical task focus on the elucidation of what is hidden and obscure. Indeed, the criteria of elucidation demand that interpretation not be equated with transliteration, which is not the equivalent of translation since it refuses to engage in the

[1]Cf. James M. Robinson, "Hermeneutic Since Barth," *The New Hermeneutic*, ed. J. M. Robinson and J. B. Cobb, Jr. (New Frontiers In Theology vol. 2; New York: Harper & Row, 1964) 1–7.

risk that is inherent in every form of translation. G. Ebeling makes some pertinent observations on this issue:

> Not only does the translation remain imperfect with respect to the original text, always lagging behind the original, but every translation also remains a part of the historical past, since every living language is involved in change. The meanings of words change, concepts (*die Begriffe*) deteriorate in the course of time, becoming (as we say) "worn out," having lost their earlier capacity for expression (*Aussage-gehalt*) and the power that was once theirs. Man in this world of his [*sic*], however, is a historical being [*der geschictliche Mensch*], caught up with the world in constant change, a being whose present life cannot be repeated, and who must therefore be addressed and confronted as the one he is now in his world—the only way in which we can say today, in a strict sense, what was said in the past is to say it today in a new and different way. The sermon must be interpretation because the world of Holy Scripture is historical, because proclamation is a historical process, and because the persons to whom proclamation is addressed are historical along with their world. Therefore theology necessarily always finds itself involved in constant change. There can be no *theologia perennis* and even the historical reality of the church is necessarily subjected to continuous change.[2]

And so these chapters aim at a conception of the hermeneutical task that focuses on its historical-theological meaning rather than on its historical-archaeological location. In short, rather than dealing with the classical "introductory" questions—who, what, when, where, and how?—these lectures will focus primarily on literary and theological questions, such as context (where?), flow of the argument (how?), precision of the argument (what?), and the punchline of the text and its relevance (so what?).

---

[2]Gerhard Ebeling, *The Problem of Historicity in the Church and Its Proclamation*, trans. G. Foley (Philadelphia: Fortress Press, 1967) 22–23, 25–27.

CHAPTER 2

Paul's First Letter to the Corinthians

Overall Structure of the Letter

    A. Salutation, 1:1-3

    B. Thanksgiving, 1:4-9

    C. Response to oral reports about communal conflicts and ethical misconduct, 1:10—6:20

    D. Response to written questions by the Corinthians, 7:1—16:12

        1. Marriage, chap. 7

        2. Meat offered to idols, chaps. 8–10

        3. Worship and the Eucharist, chap. 11

        4. Spiritual gifts, chaps. 12–14

        5. The resurrection of the body, chap. 15

        6. The collection for the saints in Jerusalem, chap. 16

    E. Greeting, 16:13-24

Literary Observations

THE INVESTIGATION OF THE OVERALL STRUCTURE OF A PAULINE letter is quite similar to that of an individual section within the letter. The same questions apply, albeit on a larger scale. They concern:

    a. The relation of the whole to the parts: How do the parts constitute the whole and how does the whole relate to the individual parts?

    b. What is the basic movement of the argument that pervades the letter and section as a whole?

    c. What is the essential punchline or thematic focus that holds the various sections of the letter or section together? In the case of 1 Corinthians, these questions are difficult to answer because there seems to be no thematic focus or basic unity to the letter. To illustrate the nature of the problems that 1 Corinthians presents, a comparison with Paul's Letter to the Romans may be helpful.

Romans has been called a "letter-essay" or "didactic letter."[1] Indeed, reading on the surface very much like a "dogmatics in outline" and due to its sustained coherent argument that unfolds in systematic fashion, the basic theme is presented in 1:16-17: "For I am not ashamed of the gospel: it is the power of God for salvation to everyone who has faith, to the Jew first and also to the Greek. For in it the righteousness of God is revealed through faith for faith; as it is written, 'He who is righteous will live by faith.' " The several parts of the letter are clearly held together by this basic theme, which begins to unfold in 1:18 on and reaches its climax in the doxology of 15:13. In Romans we see Paul as "the systematic thinker" at work. Thus, it is no surprise that in the history of Christian doctrine Romans was regarded as a "compendium of Christian doctrine" (Melanchthon). Indeed, we may well ask whether Romans is a letter at all. Is it directed to specific concerns of the Roman community? These questions become all the more urgent when we observe its systematic and didactic composition with its seemingly universal and timeless quality.

1 Corinthians seems to be the exact opposite of Romans. As the structural outline of the letter shows (see above), its contingent aspects are quite obvious when we notice Paul's various responses to concrete problems in the Corinthian Church. However, what is not obvious is whether the letter exhibits a sustained, coherent, and "wholistic" argument, which undergirds and unfolds a coherent, unified theme. Indeed, in contrast to the unified thematic argument of Romans, 1 Corinthians seems a composite of disconnected parts, a multiplicity of various answers to a series of diverse problems. Instead of dealing with Paul "the systematic thinker"—as in Romans—we seem to be dealing here with Paul "the problem solver," "the pastoral counselor," who is engaged in momentary, ad hoc replies to a variety of questions and specific situations.

---

[1]Karl P. Donfried, "False Presuppositions in the Study of Romans," *The Romans Debate* (Minneapolis: Augsburg, 1977) 120–48.

Where in 1 Corinthians do we find a basic theological theme that constitutes the unifying source which underlies the diverse answers Paul gives? In fact, 1 Corinthians is in many ways a "question-answer" product: oral reports from Chloe and her people about the situation in Corinth, supplemented by similar reports from Stephanas, Fortunatus, and Achaius (1:11; 16:17; cf. 5:1; 11:18) are followed by written questions from the Corinthians, which are clearly marked by the recurring clause "concerning" (*peri*): concerning marriage and celibacy (7:1); concerning virgins (7:25); concerning meat offered to idols (8:1); concerning spiritual gifts (12:1); concerning the collection (16:1); and concerning Apollos (16:12).

In other words, whereas in Romans the coherence of the argument is evident—but its contingent setting, that is, the specificity of situation, audience, and occasion is a problem—in 1 Corinthians the situational contingency is abundantly clear, but the coherence and ordering theme of the letter is problematic. Therefore, it comes as no surprise that many scholars consider 1 Corinthians to be an aggregate of several letters written at different occasions and only later conjoined by an editor.[2]

Theological Observations

BEFORE ADDRESSING THE PROBLEM OF THE THEMATIC UNITY OF 1 Corinthians—the issue of the controlling key *from* which and *to* which Paul argues—we must notice that the letter documents in a basic manner Paul's theological method. His way of "doing theology" is the way of praxis—of theological reflection on concrete, situational needs. We may call it "theology in the first mode of reflection," quite similar to what third-world theologians mean by theology as "orthopraxis" rather than as "orthodoxy." This type of theological reflection forms as well the basis of many D.Min. programs in our country, for example, a case study method of action and reflection. In other words, the *content* of Paul's thought cannot be divorced from its *function*, that is, from the manner and mode of Paul's theologizing.

To be sure, the pitfalls that accompany this way of doing theology need to be kept in mind. Situational theology cannot disintegrate into opportunistic strategies, such as keeping the church together at the cost of

---

[2]See, for example, W. Schmithals, "Die Korintherbriefe als Briefsammlung," *ZNW* 64 (1973) 263–88.

distorting the gospel. Moreover, it cannot compromise the truth of the gospel by merely appealing to the authority of its proclaimer, that is, to the charismatic voice and spellbinding person of the apostle or to his authoritarianism.

Indeed, 1 Corinthians demonstrates that whatever the basic coherent truth of the gospel is, it cannot be a docetic-abstract truth, but rather it must address whatever problems believers in Corinth face. In other words, Paul's theologizing is marked by its particularity, by his constant attempt to make the abiding word of the gospel a word on target for his audience. Thus, as I stated earlier, the *content* of Paul's gospel can never be divorced from his *hermeneutic*, that is, from the interpretive strategies that he employs to do justice to the incarnational depth of the gospel. Indeed, a homogenized version of Paul's thought that abstracts its eternal verities from its necessary application to diverse human needs and crises amounts to a misapprehension of Paul's theological intent.

Keeping in mind Paul's method of intertwining the central and abiding coherence of the gospel with the contingent circumstances of his churches, the question whether this applies to 1 Corinthians as well demands an urgent answer. For we have noticed that in this letter the relation of the multiple contingent concerns to its coherent center is not at all obvious.

Along similar lines, E. Lohse observes that "the oral and written reports and questions which came to the apostle account for the rather disconnected train of thought in the answer which he gives to the church in 1 Corinthians."[3] However, Karl Barth in his *The Resurrection of the Dead* has shown that there is after all "a canon within the canon in the letter." He argues that all the diverse contingent questions are held together by the resurrection chapter (chapter 15). He suggests that chapter 15 is not only the climax of the letter in its literary structure, but forms as well the basic theological ground for Paul's argument with the Corinthians concerning all the other issues that are raised in the letter. Thus, Barth posits chapter 15 as the coherent center of the letter.[4] In support of Barth's contention, we can point to the thanksgiving clause in 1:4-9 which, according to P. Schubert's investigation, forms the clue to the

[3]Eduard Lohse, *The Formation of the New Testament*, trans. M. E. Boring (Nashville: Abingdon, 1981) 67.
[4]Karl Barth, *The Resurrection of the Dead* (New York: Fleming H. Revell, 1933) 13–124.

theme of a letter.[5] Indeed, the thanksgiving clause of 1 Corinthians epit-
omizes the content of the letter as a whole:

> 1:5a "In every way, you have been enriched
>   in him in speech" (*logos*: wisdom motif)   chapters 1–4
> 1:5b (in) "knowledge" (*gnosis*) of every kind   chapters 8–10
> 1:7a "so that you are not lacking in any
>   spiritual gift" (*charisma*)   chapters 12–14
> 1:7b-9 "as you wait for the revealing of
>   our Lord Jesus Christ"   chapter 15

Chapter 15: The Key to the Letter

The Theology of the Corinthians. If chapter 15 is indeed the underlying
center of the letter, what does it reveal and why is this chapter so central
to Paul's argument?

The cogency of Paul's argument depends on the adequacy of his response to the theological challenge that the Corinthians present to him.
In other words, we must understand the "text" of the Corinthian Christians before we can grasp the bite of Paul's "contra-text" in its diverse
expressions. In doing so, we must not forget that a letter is like a tele-
phone conversation of which we hear only one side. What, then, can we
learn from Paul's response in 1 Corinthians 15 about the position of the
Corinthians?

The Corinthians refused to accept the future resurrection of the dead:
"Now if Christ is proclaimed as raised from the dead, how can some of
you say there is no resurrection of the dead?" (15:12). Note that the
Corinthians did not deny the resurrection of Christ, on which they in fact
based their Christian life, but rather considered a future resurrection of
bodies not only unnecessary but also unintelligible and disgusting.

a. It was not necessary because Paul had taught them that Christian
existence means to be "in Christ"—to have been crucified and raised
with Christ. In other words, to be "in Christ" means that we have already been raised with Christ and thus enjoy Christ's victory over the
evil powers of sin and death by our incorporation and sacramental union
with him. Thus, spiritually speaking, sin and death have been overcome.

---

[5]Paul Schubert, *Form and Function of the Pauline Thanksgivings* (BZNW 20;
Giessen/Berlin: Töpelmann, 1939).

Because Paul had spoken to them about the evil world, from which Christ has liberated us, Christians are spiritually free from involvement in this world. They now live on a new plane; enjoy the gift of the Spirit, along with the gifts of wisdom and *gnōsis* (insight). Consequently, Christian mission to the world consists in exhibiting to the world what knowledge of Christ means, namely speaking in the language of angels (*glossolalia*, chaps. 13 and 14); and demonstrating the power of healing (12:9). For all this shows that spiritual perfection is nothing but a pure gift of grace. After all, Christ was not sent into our world to introduce dialectics, ambiguities, and paradoxes of the "yes-but" variety; rather he came to give us fullness of life, a supreme transforming moment, so that we might have a full knowledge of the richness of the gospel (1:5). And this means that, although we still must live in this world, our spiritual life cannot be affected by it. Christians are indeed self-consciously and proudly marginal people in the world!

b. Moreover, a resurrection of bodies is not only unnecessary and unintelligible but also disgusting, because a future resurrection of bodies means a negation of our spiritual bliss. As every good Greek knows, the material body is fundamentally a transient entity and ties us to this evil, temporary world. It simply cannot participate in spiritual reality. For what has my true self to do with my bodily liabilities? Plato had already stated that "the body is a tomb" (*sōma sēma*). Indeed, the body cannot be spiritually significant for it is in every way opposed to real life in the Spirit. Therefore, Spirit and matter and Spirit and body cannot be conjoined. And so the Corinthians say: "Our apostle Paul was certainly our 'father in Christ' " (4:15); but what gives him the right to impose on us his own cultural ideology, that is, his Jewish apocalyptic worldview with its dogma of the resurrection of the body? To be sure, Jewish tradition can neither conceive of a self without a body nor contemplate eternal life without a resurrection of the body, but that really obscures the essence of the gospel by overlaying it with unnecessary Jewish supplements. How can Paul claim so ardently that a Gentile does not need to become a Jew *physically* (by circumcision) in order to gain a full Christian status, and yet insist that a Gentile must become a Jew *mentally* and *intellectually* before he can become a Christian by accepting an alien, Jewish worldview? That simply does not fit a man who claims to be the supreme "apostle of the Gentiles" (Romans 11:13). Above all, Paul must be able to translate the one gospel into a variety of worldviews. When Harry Emerson Fosdick calls the gospel an abiding experience amidst changing worldviews, and when Bultmann's demythologizing program aims to clarify the gospel for the sake of its kerygmatic impact on our contemporary world, Paul certainly seems to transgress this task. When Paul claims our freedom in Christ as the highest fruit of the gospel, then he cannot contaminate this freedom as he does by imposing on us an ideological, Jewish worldview. Moreover, he cannot locate our full richness in Christ in some future life to come by making the future resurrection of the dead an essential part of the gospel.

Indeed, the Corinthians claimed to be the "now" generation in Christ: what counts is the "now" of our new creation in Christ. Since we are anchored in the now, the now is not to be dislocated in some speculative future, as if the present hour is only a dialectical mixture of "the already, but not yet," a state of being both sinners and yet justified (cf. Luther, *simul iustus ac peccator*).

Paul's Response to the Corinthians. Paul's response to the Corinthians is directed at their spiritual perfectionism. He often cites important elements of their thought: "all of us possess knowledge" (8:1); and surely "all things are lawful for me" (6:12; 10:23); indeed "food is meant for the stomach and the stomach for food, and God will destroy both one and the other" (6:13). We must understand that Paul's attack is based on two basic components of his gospel: the *transcendent character* of God's sovereignty over creation and the *universal purpose* of God's saving action in Christ. Therefore, in order to safeguard God's transcendent character, Paul insists on *conjoining* what the Corinthians want to *disjoin*, namely, the relation of the Spirit and the body. Moreover, in order to safeguard God's universal purpose of redemption, he insists on *disjoining* what the Corinthians desire to *conjoin*, namely, the conflation and fusion of the saving realities of the present with those of the future, when God's kingdom will embrace his whole creation. Thus, Paul counters their elitist spiritualism by arguing that our present status in Christ signifies the first-fruits of God's coming kingdom, not the whole harvest (15:20-28) and that our present union with the risen Lord depends on a cruciform life in the midst of the realities of this world rather than a disdainful escape from this world, prematurely celebrating the fullness of salvation.

In other words, Paul insists on correlating the Spirit and the body because what is essential to his gospel is the relevance of moral action in the body—our deed in the historical world as inspired by the Spirit.

Moreover, what the Corinthians reject as a purely ideological cultural in-trusion in the gospel—that is, the apocalyptic Jewish worldview with its hope in God's coming triumph over the world—is for Paul the indispensible means to express a crucial theological issue because it means that Christians are not "untouchables" in Christ or the *beati possidentes* (people who have got it made), but rather instruments in God's universal redemptive plan for the world. We may add that in this respect the Corinthians are people very much like us, rejecting ambiguities in favor of realized eschatologies!

Conclusion

THE CORINTHIANS VIEWED THE CHURCH AS A "SPIRITUALISTIC ghetto" that has closed its windows to the world; as if it were an end in itself rather than a means for God's redemptive plan with his world. They lacked reality-awareness, which substitutes the church as a spiritual utopia for a conception of the church as a militant community of pilgrims on the way to the kingdom of God.

Their ecclesiology operated with a radical dualism between the sacred and the secular and was committed to an individualistic anthropology, which looks at individuals as spiritualized selves-in-isolation. And so the Corinthians betray not only a communal conception of the church, but also its solidarity with a world in need of redemption. Consequently, the Corinthians despised entanglements with the "body" and "bodily" matters, that is, with the ethical issues that the world presented to them. Thus, it comes as no surprise that a basic ethical and communal threat runs through all of Paul's so diverse answers in the letter.

In short, the Corinthians were committed to the slogan "spirituality and materiality" (that is, bodily involvement) do not mix. Faith spiritually lifts us above historical entanglements, above the realities of our world. Indeed, Paul's counterattack makes sense against this background: while the Corinthians divorced Spirit and body, Paul conjoins them as inherent in the truth of the gospel. And so he tells them:

Spiritual life is *in* the body and never apart from it. It is *for* other bodies as it comes to concrete expression in the church which Paul calls "the body of Christ" (cf. 3:16; 6:13-20; 9:27; 12:12-28). It is noteworthy that in no other letter of Paul do the concepts of body (*sōma*) and Spirit (*pneuma*) appear so frequently as in 1 Corinthians ("body" appears forty times and "Spirit"/"spiritual" forty-five times).

The church as the body of Christ is indeed constituted as one body that honors pluriformity and diversity of each member. Therefore, all members each possess their own specific spiritual gift (*charisma*). Indeed, a body is only a body when all its members together execute their necessary function.

The body of Christ is not to be equated with the fullness of the coming glory and triumph of God. Rather, it functions as the beachhead of God's dawning kingdom in the world. Indeed, the church is in a situation of struggle and temptation (cf. 10:1-13) as long as the power of death reigns in the world (15:26). Only when death has lost its grip on God's creation will his kingdom be realized. Its manifestation does not mean the annihilation of God's created order, but rather its transformation. Therefore, Paul insists on the future resurrection of the dead because it signals the redemption of the whole person—body and spirit—and thus rejects the notion of the immortality of the individual soul.

As Christians we live *now* in Christ while we *hope* for God's coming victory. Only then "the perfect comes and the imperfect will pass away" (13:10 RSV). To live now in Christ means to live by the Spirit in the body for other bodies; but we live in the hope of becoming "spiritual bodies" at the time of the resurrection of the dead.

And so the resurrection argument of 1 Corinthians 15 thematizes all the diverse answers that Paul renders in 1 Corinthians. It is indeed the red thread that connects its various parts. It does so in a twofold way: first, the stress on the resurrection body shows that life in the body for other bodies is inseparable from life in the Spirit because the deeds of the body have eternal significance for our participation in the coming kingdom of God. Second, the future dimension of the kingdom of God and of the resurrection of the dead means that our union with Christ in our present life is not only a gift, but also a mandate (15:58). The future dimension of God's kingdom alerts us to the fact that Christian life is not a completed life, because it must wait for the redemption of all of God's creatures in the world in God's own time.

CHAPTER 3

Paul's Second Letter to the Corinthians

Overall Structure of the Letter

A. Preface, 1:1-2
B. A Review of Paul's Past Experience, 1:3-11
C. Transition to the Letter's First Theme, 1:12-14
D. Paul's Self-Defense of His Travel Plans, 1:15—2:3
E. The Main Theme: Paul's Apostolic Ministry, 2:14—6:13 and 7:2-16
F. An Interpolation, 6:14—7:1
G. The Collection, 8:1—9:15
H. "The Letter of Tears," 10:1—13:10
I. Greeting, 13:11-13

R. P. Martin writes: "Where the contents of 1 Corinthians fall into well-defined sections, . . . in 2 Corinthians the flow of Paul's writing is erratic and less well ordered, especially in the first seven chapters."[1] The composition of the letter is even more erratic than Martin allows. There are obvious breaks at 2:13, 6:13, and 10:1, and chapters 8 and 9, which deal with Paul's collection for Jerusalem, are out of place in the letter. Although my outline resembles that of Martin, I have adopted Bornkamm's suggestion that 2 Corinthians consists of a number of separate letters that have been compiled by an editor.[2]

---

[1] Ralph P. Martin, *2 Corinthians* (WBC 40; Waco, Tex.: Word Books, 1985) xxv.
[2] Günther Bornkamm, "Die Vorgeschichte des sogennanten Zweiten Korintherbriefes," *Gesammelte Aufsätze,* (BEvT 53; Munich: C. Kaiser, 1971) 4. 162–94.

Therefore, I propose the following chronological composition of the letter:

2:14—6:13; 7:2-4 comprises Paul's "Letter of Defense," which he sent along with Titus to Corinth in order to deal with the influence of itinerant Christian missionaries who had invaded the church and challenged Paul's authority.

10:1—13:13—the "Letter of Tears" (cf. 2:4), which Paul wrote in defense of his apostolic work after having been rejected by the Corinthians on a previous visit.

1:1—2:13; 7:5-16—the "Letter of Reconciliation" which Paul wrote after Titus had returned with the news of the Corinthians' renewed allegiance to Paul.

8:1—9:5—the "Collection Letters."

6:14—7:1—an exhortation to loyalty centered in Paul's teaching; added by a redactor.

The Gospel according to Paul's Opponents in Corinth

PAUL'S SECOND LETTER TO THE CORINTHIANS RESEMBLES in many ways his Letter to the Galatians. In both letters the emotional and passionate person of the apostle comes to the surface. They are occasioned by the bitter attack of his opponents on the authenticity of his apostolate. Indeed, in both letters Paul "wears his heart on his sleeve and speaks without constraint, hiding neither his affection, nor his anger, nor his agony."[3]

However, notwithstanding the fact that the personality of Paul in all its dimensions comes into clearer focus in Galatians and 2 Corinthians than in any of his other letters, the attacks on his apostolate center on different issues in these two letters. In Galatia, Paul is charged with distorting the "Jerusalem gospel," because his law-free gospel is attributed to his deviance from the gospel of the mother church in Jerusalem. In 2 Corinthians, however, the relation of law and gospel does not lie behind the attack on Paul's apostolate nor does the letter use Paul's terminology of justification as in Galatians. The focus here is Paul's personal status and

---

[3]C. K. Barrett, *The Second Epistle to the Corinthians* (HNTC; New York: Harper & Row, 1973) 32.

apostolic behavior. He is charged with a lack of "personal presence," spiritual greatness, and missionary effectiveness, thereby demonstrating that he is not qualified to be an apostle. How can a man whose life is so unspectacular and whose actions are so inconspicuous claim to be an apostle of "the gospel of the glory of Christ" (4:4)? Paul is simply "weak" and unimpressive, for he himself admits, "I do not want to seem as though I am trying to frighten you with my letters. For they say, 'His letters are weighty and strong, but his bodily presence is weak, and his speech contemptible' " (10:9-10). Rather than embodying the victory of Christ over the powers of this world, he seems subject to them. Although he claims to be an accredited apostle, he cannot in any sense be called a personal disciple of Jesus. Consequently, his message about Christ is not informed by the knowledge of Jesus' own glorious ministry (5:16). Moreover, he shows his timidity not only in his speech and personal presence (10:10), but also in his apparent lack of self-worth and courage. He labors for his own keep and does not even claim a salary or support from his converts, as befits an apostle (12:13). Furthermore, his collection drive is probably an attempt to rob the church for personal gain (12:17-18). In short, Paul has no charisma, and there is no evidence of Christ's word and personal presence in him (13:3).

We see, then, that the contours of the charges against Paul are shaped by the picture of the apostle as a divine miracle worker, one who embodies the divine presence. His opponents probably claim to know the historical Jesus by way of their Jerusalem connections, a knowledge that centers on Jesus' miracles and signs. Indeed, they claim that Jesus still communicates his powerful presence to those who belong to him and enables them to rise above the world by demonstrating his victory in their pneumatic behavior. The resurrection of Jesus assures the continuation of his miraculous activity and glory in his apostles and signifies their separation from a corrupt world. The interpretation of the Old Testament apparently undergirds this picture of Jesus. In chapter 3, Jesus is portrayed as the true successor of Moses — not as the new lawgiver (cf. Matthew), but as the initiator into divine glory. The opposition, then, interprets Moses as Philo does in his *Life of Moses*, where the epiphany of the divine transforms human beings into "divine men" and/or "royal prophets."

Although the interpretation of 2 Corinthians 3 as a reworked midrash (cf. D. Georgi) remains conjectural, the prominent use of the name of the historical Jesus in 4:5, 10, 11, 14 and 11:4 — so rare elsewhere in the letters of Paul (cf. Rom. 3:26; 1 Cor. 12:3; 1 Thess. 4:14) — gives credence to the presence of a "Jesus theology" in Corinth.[4] The reference to "another Jesus," "a different Spirit," and "a different gospel" (11:4), along with that to "knowing Christ according to the flesh" (5:16; translation mine), points to a type of "Divine Man" Christology (*theios anēr*) and to a gospel that consists of an aretology of Jesus. Jesus' divine status is here disclosed in his prophetic, miraculous activity, which is confirmed by his resurrection. In this manner, the true disciple-apostle is viewed as embodying the epiphany of Jesus on earth. The Corinthian apostles subscribe to the slogan, "The Christian message succeeds because it works." Its effectiveness is demonstrable in the works of these apostles, that is, in their "signs and wonders and mighty works" (12:12). They boast about their missionary success (10:15; 11:10) and carry with them letters of recommendation (3:1), so as to recommend themselves as evidence of the truth of the gospel.

In addition to their "boasting" and "self-recommendation" (5:12), they call themselves "servants of Christ" (*diakonoi Christou*; 11:23). Paul uses this terminology nowhere so frequently and emphatically as in this letter (cf. 3:6; 6:4; 11:15, 23; cf. also "service" [*diakonia*] in 3:7-9; 4:1; 5:18; 6:3; 8:4; 9:1, 12-13; 11:8; and "to serve" [*diakonein*] in 3:3; 8:19). Because Paul prefers elsewhere the prophetic (Old Testament) title "slave/servant of Christ" (*doulos Christou*) as his self-designation (Rom. 1:1; Gal. 1:10), he probably borrows the title *diakonos Christou* from the Corinthian apostles and applies it to himself (11:23). However, the precise meaning of the term remains unclear. It probably refers to their mystic knowledge of Christ (11:6) and their union with him (13:3), because these apostles demonstrate as "servants of Christ" the success of a follower of Jesus (11:12) and radiate his divine glory.

Paul's Response

PAUL IS CLEARLY ON THE DEFENSIVE IN CORINTH, FOR NOTHING succeeds like success. And yet, or possibly because of it, his polemic is here even sharper than in Galatians. In Corinth there is as well a "different gospel," a pseudo-gospel preached by pseudo-apostles (2 Cor. 11:13; cf. Gal. 1:6-9). Paul attacks his opponents by focusing on the cruciform nature of Christian existence, in contrast to their view of it as empirically

---

[4]Dieter Georgi, *The Opponents of Paul in Second Corinthians* (Philadelphia: Fortress Press, 1986).

victorious and glorious. His underlying theme comes to the fore in 13:4, "Christ was crucified in weakness, but lives by the power of God. For we are weak in him, but in dealing with you we will live with him by the power of God." What is at stake for Paul is the nature of the victory of Christ as it embodies itself in his apostolic experience in the world. And how different Romans is from 2 Corinthians in its reflection on Paul's apostolic life and on Christian existence! The meditative, argumentative mood of Romans comes to expression in 2 Corinthians (especially in chapters 10–13) in a charged experiential and emotional manner. Chapters 10–13 do not contain sustained theological reflections on the relationship of Christology to anthropology and ethics (cf. Romans 5–8). Paul speaks viscerally here, and his hermeneutic of the gospel is carried out with experiential intensity. The human limitations and grandeur of the apostle explode here before our eyes. These chapters exhibit Paul's personal piety and praxis, and they reveal more about his "soul" than any psychological speculation about the circumstances of his conversion.

Conflict is inherent in piety when it serves the world. Anger and frustration combine with pride; emotional outbursts climax in joyful peace. Paul is nowhere more angry than when his own churches pervert the gospel. In fact, his indictment of the pagan world—which hardly fills the pages of his letters—seems mild compared to his indictment of fellow Christians who pervert the gospel. Such an indictment is surprising when we remember the sociopolitical situation of the church in the Roman world: a sociological and religious minority attempts to establish its identity apart from Judaism and Hellenistic-Roman society, with its ethnic religions and "ecumenical cults" (cf. the popular mystery religion of Isis "with the thousand names"). In this situation of hostility, persecution, and legal insecurity, every brother and sister counts in order to secure a certain cohesiveness in the Christian movement. Tolerance and unity in the rank and file are crucial for survival. Why, then, this dangerous intolerance of Paul to the opposition, especially when it is sociologically so destructive? The answer to this is that Paul cannot compromise the truth of the gospel.

Exhibition of religious pride and flaunting one's union with Christ is, according to Paul, nothing but worship of "Satan" (11:14), and thus a radical perversion of the gospel. The historical Jesus and his resurrection are here appropriated by the Corinthian apostles as miraculous transformation and religious success in the world. The gospel thus creates the "superman." Both the "not yet" of the apocalyptic hope and the relation of the resurrection to the cross of Christ are undone. The coming age of glory is inserted into this world as an enclave for the pneumatic elite, and the cross is viewed as incidental to the glory of the resurrection. It seems as if the Corinthians base their theology on the "superman Jesus" as portrayed in a section of Mark's Gospel (chapters 3–9), while they omit Mark's passion story! For Paul, however, the resurrection of Christ confirms the cross in that it establishes Christian life "in weakness" (13:4) and in a cruciform existence until the time of the apocalyptic resurrection of the dead (4:10, 17-18; 5:4-10). The disjunction between the death and resurrection of Christ, and our own future resurrection, means that in this world the resurrection manifests itself as the victory of the cross, i.e., as "power in weakness" (12:8-10). Thus, we "always" carry "in the body the death of Jesus" (4:10) and are called to redemptive suffering for the sake of the world (4:12). A cruciform lifestyle, then, is the inevitable consequence of the confession, "I have been crucified with Christ" (Gal. 2:19), because it means a glorying "in the cross of our Lord Jesus Christ, by which the world has been crucified to me, and I to the world" (Gal. 6:14; cf. Phil. 3:9). Cruciform apostolic experience is not a form of masochism or a rejoicing in passion mysticism, because it translates itself as sobriety for the sake of the public accountability and the intelligible character of the gospel over against private ecstasy. It is remarkable that Paul—having to compete with the pneumatic pride and success of his opponents—elevates the upbuilding of the church over any display of ecstatic exhibitionism: "For if we are beside ourselves, it is for God; if we are in our right mind (cf. *La Sainte Bible de Jerusalem* (1956): '*raisonables*'), it is for you." In other words, Paul's passion is not simply an outburst of self-serving, pneumatic exuberance; rather, his passion is the passion of compassion. For the sober apostolic "reasonableness" of Paul is motivated by his pastoral concern for the Corinthians. Thus, cruciform existence translates itself as affliction and hardship for the sake of the gospel (4:7-12; 6:3-10; 12:7-10), or as "the daily pressure upon me because of my anxiety for all the churches" (11:28), or as refusing pay (11:9; 12:13) so as not to be "an obstacle to" the truth of the gospel (6:3). Above all, it means to recognize the distinction between "the transcendent power of God" and "the earthen vessel" of the apostle (4:7). In 2 Corinthians God's power in Christ is primarily viewed as "weakness" (12:10) and as "the sufferings of Christ" (1:3-7), which conforms to the cruciform signature of apostolic experience, and is especially documented in the so-called "pericopes of crisis" (*peristaseis*) of 4:8-12, 6:4-10, and 11:23-29. In this letter the dialectic of cross and resurrection seems to overshadow the marks of the presence of resurrection-life in this world by the power of the Spirit. And yet the cruciform existence of the apostle and the Corinthians alike is lived in the expectation of the final triumph and judgment of God, and of the life of the resurrection after death (4:10-11; 5:1-10; 11:2-3, 15; 13:4).

2 Corinthians, then, demonstrates the experiential reality of "the mortal body" of the apostle, both in its subjection to death (1:8-10) and in its redemptive activity in the world (4:10-12).

And so the boasting of the apostle reaches its climax in the confession "Whenever I am weak, then I am strong" (12:10), which comes as the counterpoint to all his previous boastings and marks them as foolish (11:6—12:6).

To be sure, Paul believes in "the triumphant march" of the gospel in the world (2:14-16). He shares this conviction with all the New Testament authors, especially Luke-Acts. But unlike Luke-Acts, Paul views the mode of this victory in a different way. For unlike Luke-Acts, the world does not come out to hear him when he arrives in a city, and it is not impressed by his personality. Rather, the victory of the gospel is that of the grace of God in Christ that contradicts both the world and our own strength (1:12; 10:13; 12:9), and yet establishes beachheads of God's dawning new world in the midst of the old world. Thus, in the light of the hope that yearns for the victory of the new age (4:17; 5:1-10), victory in this life is comfort *in the midst of* suffering, and grace and power *in the midst of* weakness.

And so the death of Jesus incarnates itself in the apostle's life-giving activity (4:7-12), because he knows that resurrection-power translates itself in this world not only as passive suffering in hope, but also as active redemptive suffering.

CHAPTER 4

Paul's Letter to the Galatians

IN MOVING FROM THE CORINTHIAN CORRESPONDENCE OF PAUL TO his Letter to the Galatians, we must be aware that in the history of interpretation Galatians has often been called "the little edition of the letter to the Romans." Indeed, in descriptions of Paul's thought, Galatians frequently functions as the hermeneutical supplement and helpmate to Romans because while both letters betray a similarity of vocabulary and themes, Romans is much more explicit and extensive than Galatians. Both letters seem to set forth a unified theme that has been considered Paul's true doctrinal center: justification by faith apart from the works of the law. Moreover, there is good reason to conflate Galatians with Romans in a systematic treatment of Paul's thought. The similarity of themes and vocabulary and the analogous movement from justification by faith in the first chapters to sacramental participation in Christ and to ethical exhortation in the later chapters (cf. Gal. 1–4; 5–6; Rom. 1–5; 6–8; 12–15), suggests a unitary treatment of the two letters that can ignore incidental historical circumstances and particularity of context.

However, it is a mistake to treat Galatians and Romans as timeless, abstract products of Paul's thought. In both Galatians and Romans Paul is involved in contextual theology, that is, doing theology in such a way that the situation of the audience in each letter determines the texture of Paul's arguments and thought.

Overall Structure of the Letter

I. Prescript, 1:1-5
II. Body of Letter, 1:6—6:10
    A. The Situation, 1:6-12
    B. The Explication, 1:13—6:10
        1. Paul's gospel is not derived "from a human source" (*para anthropou*), 1:13—2:21
        2. Paul's gospel is not "of human origin" (*kata anthrōpon*), but is "according to Scripture" (*kata tēn graphēn*), 3:1—5:12
            a. Appeal to Christian Experience, 3:1-5
            b. The Witness of Scripture, 3:6-18
            c. The True Function of the Law, 3:19—4:7
            d. Renewed Appeal to the Galatians, 4:8-20
            e. The Witness of Scripture, 4:21-31
            f. Appeal to the Galatians to Stand in Freedom, 5:1-12
        3. Ethic of Freedom in Love through the Spirit, 5:13—6:10
            a. Christian Freedom as Service, 5:13-15
            b. Christian Life in the Spirit, 5:16-25
            c. Warning against Conceit, 5:26—6:6
            d. Exhortation, 6:7-10
III. Postscript, 6:11-18

The Theology of the Galatians

THE GALATIANS, WHO WERE GENTILES LIVING IN THE TERRITORY OF Asia Minor called Galatia, became converts due to Paul's missionary activity. After his last visit to them (Acts 18:23), itinerant Jewish–Christian missionaries had come in to correct Paul's presentation of the gospel (1:7; 4:17; 5:10; 6:12). The situation resembles that which prevails in 2 Corinthians, where Jewish-Christian missionaries had invaded the Corinthian Church with a "different Jesus" and a "different gospel" (2 Cor. 11:4). In Galatia the Jewish-Christian missionaries were able—to Paul's astonishment—to convince the Galatians of the truth of their cause. How did they manage to make such a convincing appeal? To be sure, the opponents did not intend to apostatize from the gospel; they merely wanted to perfect what Paul had "commenced" (3:3). In order to discredit Paul's gospel, they devised a strategy that combined personal attack and theological polemics. If they could undermine Paul's apostolate, they could undermine his gospel as well. Thus, they forced Paul into a personal defense of his person. Indeed, the defense of his apostolate is Paul's primary concern in Galatians, just as it is in 2 Corinthians (chapters 10–13), for if this fails, the truth of his gospel is likewise surrendered.

And so Paul must defend both his apostolic status and the truth of the gospel (1:1-12). The argument of the opponents runs along the following lines: You Galatians were Gentiles when, through the gospel that Paul preached, you turned to Christ. This turning away from idols and "the elemental spirits of the universe" (4:3, 9) is an important first step. It is like the step Gentiles take when they turn from idols to the God of Israel and attach themselves as semi-proselytes or God-fearers to the synagogue.

However, do not mistake the first step for the end of the road (3:3). Paul misled you when he told you that your new status as sons of God in Christ depends on faith alone. That is an opportunistic misconstruction of the gospel and undermines its full implications. You realize, of course, that our Christ was the Messiah, who was promised to the people of Israel, the true sons of Abraham. Jesus Christ is indeed the messianic fulfillment of the promise to Abraham, and therefore the promise pertains to those who belong to the people of Israel. It does not mean that you Gentiles are excluded from the promise. You can participate in the full blessings promised to Abraham if you join the people of the promise.

When Paul contrasts the Torah (the Law) with Christ, he is not only wrong but also opportunistic, because he intends to make it religiously and sociologically easy for Gentiles to become Christians in order to enhance his apostolic grandeur. It is simply false that Gentiles can remain participants in pagan society without the "yoke of the Torah." The Torah and Christ cohere, because it is only within the realm of the Torah that the promise to Abraham is fulfilled in Christ.

To be sure, the observance of the Torah does not mean the observance of all its statutes and ordinances (cf. "the whole law" [5:3, 14; 6:13]). Although Jesus Christ, the Messiah, acknowledged their validity, they have been fulfilled in his death for us. Nevertheless, 'Torah-keeping' means the obligation to become a member of the Jewish people and therefore circumcision marks your entrance into the line of salvation-history that started with Abraham and finds its fulfillment in Christ. The Torah, then, has primarily salvation-historical significance; it assures your participation in Christ by placing you in the correct salvation-historical scheme. What counts is its cultic-cosmic meaning as law of the universe. Therefore, circumcision and Jewish calendar observances (4:10) will complete your status as full Christians and guarantee God's divine blessing upon you as the sons of Abraham.

Paul should have taught you the gospel in this way. His claim to apostolic independence is actually a combination of opportunism and disobedience. His opportunism aims at painless mass conversions that serve to enhance his ego, whereas his disobedience is apparent when he—contrary to directions from Jewish-Christian headquarters in Jerusalem—preaches an *abbreviated gospel*. He should have behaved in accordance with his real status and told you that he was an apostle in dependence upon Jerusalem and consequently he should have preached to you the proper and authentic gospel as he was taught it. Instead, this latecomer to the apostolic circle acts illegitimately and disobediently when he preaches a gospel that rests on *sola fide*, ignores the law and the Jewish antecedents of the Messiah, destroys the continuity of Israel with the church, and lacks a proper ethic. The Jerusalem apostles are the true authority in the church, because they were the disciples of the historical Jesus (2:6) and thus provide the continuity between Israel and the church. Therefore, they are "the acknowledged pillars" (2:9) of the new Christian temple and the true source of Paul's apostolate, as his relation to Jerusalem in the past clearly shows (1:16–2:10).

Paul's Response

THE POLEMICAL, EMOTIONAL, OFFICIAL, AND ALMOST IMPERSONAL character of Paul's response is evident both in his extensive and aggressive introduction and in omitting his customary laudatory attributes in the preface.

Thus, Paul omits the thanksgiving in the opening section of the letter and ends the letter abruptly (6:17) without greetings from coworkers or news about them. The passionate tone of the letter is evident in its literary style: apologetic self-defense (1:10—2:10); accusation (2:11-21); attack (3:1-5); scriptural midrash (3:6-14); allegorical interpretation (4:21-31) intermixed with tender appeal; sorrow (4:12-20); and bitter sarcasm (5:12).

Paul intends to dismantle the opposition by arguing for both the integrity of his apostolate and his gospel. This is evident in the literary structure of the letter (see above). In 1:11-12, he states the twofold theme: "the gospel that was proclaimed by me is not of human origin (*kata anthrōpon*); For I did not receive it from a human source (*para anthrōpou*), nor was I taught it, but I received it through a revelation about Jesus Christ" (my translation).

This twofold theme is subsequently unfolded drastically in 1:13—5:25:

"*The apostle*" (1:13—2:21). Paul's gospel does not derive "from a human source" (*para anthrōpou*); indeed, it is directly from God, and this divine origin of the gospel constitutes his apostleship.

"*The gospel*" (3:1—5:25). Paul's gospel is not "according to human standards" (*kata anthrōpon*); indeed, it is according to the Scripture of God (*kata graphēn*; 3:1—4:31) and verified by the Spirit (5:1-25).

"The apostle" (1:13—2:21). The crisis situation that Paul faces in Galatia dictates the form and substance of the argument with its sharp antitheses and invective dialogue. Paul aims at an either/or decision, because in the face of the impending defection of the church (4:11, 19), he knows that all is either won or lost. However, he carefully steers a course between an image of himself as a defector from Jerusalem and as a dependent servant of Jerusalem because he wants to demonstrate not only the independence of his apostleship and gospel, but also the basic agreement between Jerusalem and himself (1:13—2:21).

But how can he accomplish this? How can he argue agreement and not dependence, and how can he argue freedom and not rebellion? He tells his readers that his opponents distort the truth about his relations with the Jerusalem church: He is neither dependent on Jerusalem nor in disagreement with it. For his call came directly from God (1:15-16) and, apart from a fourteen-day visit with Peter three years later, he had no contact with Jerusalem but preached the gospel in Syria and Cilicia (1:16-24). Moreover, Paul's law-free gospel was acknowledged by the so-called "pillars" in Jerusalem (2:6-10). We may well ask why is Paul so much engaged in personal defense and self-legitimation? Why did he not negate himself and concentrate instead on the substance of the gospel? However, it is the nature of the attack on Paul in Galatia that compels his particular response. He is forced to authenticate himself in this situation, because the truth of the gospel in Galatia stands or falls with the truth of his apostolate. Paul cannot say, "Forget about me; only the gospel counts." The gospel and its bearer are interlocked, because if Paul is discredited in Galatia—as he is—the only gospel that remains is "the different gospel" which, in fact, is "no gospel" (1:6). The bearer of the gospel becomes all important in Galatians, because the issue is the true gospel, as opposed to the pseudo-gospel and because the apostle is responsible for the truth of the gospel against the lie.

Paul's self-defense, then, shifts into a demonstration of his exemplary apostolic life. Because he lives the truth of the gospel (4:12-15; cf. 2:14 and 5:1-2), he becomes the apostolic paradigm for the Galatians. The correlation of apostle and gospel, which dominates 1:12—2:21, continues to be a prominent theme in 3:1—5:25 when Paul moves from personal to material considerations.

"The Gospel" (3:1—5:25). Paul's argument for the gospel as preached by him focuses on the antithesis between law and gospel. It is largely based on an interpretation of Scripture (3:6-18; 4:21-31). Whereas the Galatians desire to synthesize Abraham, Torah, circumcision, and Christ, Paul drives a wedge between Abraham and the Torah, and joins Abraham to the *"pro-evangelion"* of faith for the Gentiles (3:8). Moreover, the promise of the blessing of Abraham is actualized only in Christ who, as Abraham's exclusive seed (3:16), fulfills the promise and breaks the curse of the law by his death on "the tree," so that the promise can now flow freely to the Gentiles (3:13-14). Thus, the Torah cannot be integrated into the gospel, as the Judaizers in Galatia claim. The combination of promise, Torah, circumcision, and Christ must be broken apart for the sake of "the truth of the gospel" (2:5, 14) because Christ and the Torah are contradictory principles as Hab. 2:4 and Lev. 18:5 testify (3:11-12). Thus Paul interprets salvation-history in a radically discontinuous manner—he carries out a Christocentric argument that confirms faith for the Gentiles and annuls the Torah. In fact, he claims that the Torah is simply an interloper that has asserted itself illegitimately between the promise to Abraham and its exclusive fulfillment in Christ (3:17).

Conclusion

IN TRACING PAUL'S ARGUMENT IN GALATIANS, WE MUST BE AWARE that he is facing a crisis of apostasy in which "the truth of the gospel" (2:5, 14) must prevail over the false gospel of his opponents (1:8-9). Thus Galatians is a polemical letter that demands clear-cut decisions. Paul not only argues on an either/or basis, but is also engaged in a passionate invective that causes his argument to often be cryptic and fragmentary (especially 3:19-22).

Thus, we are tempted to interpret Galatians with the help of the "so much clearer" Romans in order to bring to light the "hidden" layers beneath Paul's argument in Galatians. However, a letter written with a specific polemical purpose is not a systematic treatise. If we treat it as such, we fail to grasp the *mode* of Paul's theological thinking. Paul aims in Galatians to oppose the Judaizers, and in the process of radicalizing their position, he also radicalizes his own. Because Galatians is a first-level polemical response and not a second-level, reflective-dogmatic treatise, a fundamentally consistent picture of the argument does not emerge. The flow of the argument is complex and cryptic, as the relation between law and gospel shows. So the crisis situation in Galatia compels Paul to an argument of antithetical principles: faith versus works of the law; freedom versus slavery.

Galatians demonstrates that the interaction between theological coherence and situational particularity can lead to emphases and constructs that are clearly one-sided because they are dictated by the urgency of the situation at hand.

Thus, the Christocentrism of the Reformation's interpretation of Paul clearly depends more on its exclusive doctrinal use of Galatians than on the whole range of Paul's thought. As Luther put it, "The Epistle to the Galatians is my epistle, to which I have wedded myself. It is my Catherine von Bora."

However, when we survey the totality of Paul's thought in his several letters, we discern that it is dominated by a theocentric focus that gives his Christology a less exclusive place than is present in Galatians.

CHAPTER 5

Paul's Letter to the Romans

I shall now deal with that letter of Paul which Luther in his *Preface to Romans* characterized as "rightly the chief part of the New Testament and the clearest gospel of all." Paul's Letter to the Romans is essentially the story of the consistent continuity of God's saving plan for his world amidst and over against the discontinuity of a fallen world caused by human sinfulness. In other words, the story of Romans is the story of the continuity of the faithfulness of God (3:3) as the mark of God's self-identity and integrity.

The Faithfulness of God

THE FAITHFULNESS OF GOD MANIFESTS ITSELF IN THREE INTERRELATED phases:

First, in his continuing covenant faithfulness to his promises to Israel, so that God's original election of Israel will be vindicated by Israel's eschatological election (chapter 11). Thus, Israel's salvation-historical priority will be reaffirmed by its eschatological destiny.

Second, in his active intervention in Christ into the human situation, which is enslaved by the sins of idolatry, blindness, and guilt. The faithfulness of God—that is, his integrity—expresses itself here as the righteousness of God and as the justification of the sinner (cf. the theme of the letter in 1:16-17).

Third, in his active guidance of the church by the power of the Holy Spirit—a movement that reaches its goal in the glorification of the church and of the created world at the time of the final triumph of God, in the coming "glory of God."

Indeed, Romans reveals a cosmic dimension to God's faithfulness/ righteousness: His saving purpose is not limited to breaking down an ethnic-exclusive understanding of God's promises as understood by the Old Testament and Judaism. Indeed, the gospel not only reaches out to the Gentiles, but it also embraces God's whole creation, so that the climax of the gospel fulfills eschatologically God's purpose for his creation, its restoration to its original glory as Genesis 1:31 promised: "God saw everything that he had made, and indeed, it was very good." And so Paul proclaims that "the creation itself will be set free from its bondage to decay and will obtain the freedom of the glory of the children of God" (8:21).

We must be aware that the three phases of the faithfulness of God (see above), together with their eschatological climax, undergird the structure of Romans. This insight is all the more important when we remember how frequently the letter was dismembered in the history of Christian doctrine. Romans was not only viewed as the essence of Paul's theology, as a compendium of Christian doctrine (Melanchthon), but its "essence" was also restricted to chapters 1–5, while the other parts of the letter were either relegated to the periphery (for instance, chapters 9–11 and chapters 12–15), or deemed to be simply elaborations of chapters 1–5, such as chapters 6–8.

Especially since Luther detected in 1:17 his doctrine of justification by faith, chapters 1–5 became the main sources for Reformed faith (cf. the outlines of the *Heidelberg Catechism* and Calvin's *Institutes*). And so the Reformed doctrinal sequence of *condemnatio, contritio, justificatio,* and *sanctificatio* was derived from Romans 1–8.

Moreover, the Reformed interpretation of "the righteousness of God" in 1:17 as God's forensic act, by which he pronounces individual believers just and clothes them with the gift of righteousness, carried within itself some dangerous consequences. It singled out anthropology as the center of Paul's theology, and made individuals and their faith in Christ the exclusive focus of Paul's thought—a focus that undermined Paul's emphasis on the communal nature of the church as the body of Christ. Furthermore, its emphasis on *solus Christus* and *sola fide* promoted an ethical passivity, since the believers' total dependence on Christ made their ethical activity suspect. Such activity was always endangered by the requirement of "pure faith"—in Pauline terms by "works of the law." Indeed, the suspicion that attended the moral activity of believers led to the Lutheran doctrine of the Two Kingdoms (the kingdoms of the state and of the church), which made Christians subservient to the political powers.

Finally, we must be aware that once "righteousness" and "justification" are elevated as Paul's basic theological concepts, it becomes difficult to ensure their correct meaning. Indeed, these terms with their philosophical heritage of equity and distributive justice (Aristotle) are apt to cause us severe semantic difficulties. Their legal-forensic connotations threaten to become religiously difficult and abstract—if not unintelligible—for our religious appropriation so that we no longer feel addressed by this terminology.

Composition and Theme

IN OPPOSITION TO THE EXCLUSIVE REFORMED FOCUS OF JUSTIFICA-
tion by faith as the center of Romans, I propose the following theme for the letter in order to do justice to its rich texture: The faithfulness of God reveals itself as God's triumph in Christ over the supreme powers of sin and death and over their allies, the powers of flesh and the law. God's triumph inaugurated by his gift of righteousness in Christ will be fully actualized by God's future appearance in glory, when the creation itself will be glorified. Therefore, I outline the letter in this way:

A. Theme: God's coming triumph, 1:16-17. The gospel moves from righteousness to salvation (verse 16); it moves from righteousness to life in accordance with the promise of Habakkuk 2:4: "The one who is righteous will live by faith" (verse 17).

B. God's triumph in Christ over the power of human sin, 1:18—4:25.

C. God's triumph in Christ over the powers of sin (ch. 6), the law (ch. 7), the flesh (ch. 8) and death (5:1—8:39).

D. The necessary interdependence of Jew and Gentile in God's plan of triumph, 9:1—11:36.

E. The church and its unity as the anticipation of God's triumph, 12:1—15:13.

F. Doxology, 15:13. This forms the closure of the theme and constitutes the climax of the letter: "May the God of hope fill you with all joy and peace in believing, so that you may abound in hope by the power of the Holy Spirit."

G. The function of the apostle Paul in God's plan of triumph, 15:14—16:23.

It should be noticed that after the climactic doxology of 15:13, Paul reverts back in 15:14-33 to his reason for writing the letter and to the announcement of his forthcoming visit, an issue with which he had opened the letter in 1:1-15.

Basic Features

THE LETTER CONTAINS AT LEAST FOUR SUBSTANTIVE FEATURES:

The first feature concerns the dynamic-pulsating movement of Paul's argument. God's faithfulness is not a static quality, but rather moves toward an apocalyptic horizon — that is, the coming triumph of God. The apocalyptic horizon of the letter points to the restoration of a fallen world and to God's coming triumph over the primary powers of sin and death along with their allies, "the flesh" and "the law." For this reason, I posited the doxology of 15:13 as the climactic closure of the letter, the theme of which was announced by 1:16-17. Indeed, the content of the hope in which Christians should abound (15:13c) is the eschatological salvation, promised in 1:16. Moreover, "the power of the Spirit" (15:13d) is "the first fruit" (8:23) of the coming glory of God, whereas our "believing" (15:13b) is the foundation for our hope (5:1, 9-10, 17).

Indeed, if justification by faith would be the exclusive center of Romans, as Reformed exegesis claims, why would the letter actually continue after the discussion of the righteousness of God as justification by faith (1:18—4:25) has been concluded?

Moreover, why would Paul introduce a completely new vocabulary in 5:1-11 — a section that functions as a preface to chapters 6-8? The vocabulary of "justification" and "faith" ceases after 4:25 (it is reintroduced in chapters 9-11) and is displaced by that of "Spirit," "hope," "love," "death," and "life" — terms that do not appear in 1:18—4:25.

Therefore, the movement in Romans runs from justification to glorification — a movement to which Paul's terminology of "much more" in 5:9-10 points and which is confirmed in 8:30b: "Those whom he justified he also glorified."

The second feature of the letter focuses on Paul's apostolic mandate, which has not only a *prophetic* dimension, but also an *apocalyptic* dimension, although both dimensions are closely intertwined. The *prophetic dimension* of Paul's apostolate deals with the present situation of the church in the world and is especially evident in 1:18—4:25 (and chapters 9–11).

What is at stake in 1:18—4:25 is the issue of the unity of the church. That unity is threatened by forces in the Roman church that could destroy it. Chapters 14 and 15 demonstrate that there was bickering and dissension between Jewish and Gentile Christians over questions of the observance of kosher food and festival days, while one group in the church claims to be superior over the other. Paul addresses the situation not only pragmatically in chapters 14 and 15, but also in terms of basic theological principles in chapters 1–4. In this context Paul utters a prophetic indictment that focuses on the issue of "boasting" (2:17, 23; 3:27; 4:2). He reminds both Jews and Gentiles that their pre-Christian lives were marked by a basic equality, their captivity under the power of sin (3:9).

Only God's act of justification and grace in Christ has lifted them out of their bondage to sin and has given them their new status before God: "All have sinned and fall short of the glory of God" (3:22), and all are likewise the object of God's mercy—all alike stand or fall "by faith alone" (3:28; notice especially the emphasis on "all, everyone" [*pas*] in 3:21-31). Paul is engaged here in an intramural debate. It concerns the sociological issue of the unity of the church, the unity of Jew and Greek based solely on God's impartial verdict of judgment and mercy over both ethnic groups. Indeed, God's impartiality (2:6-11) toward Jew and Greek is an essential part of God's integrity and righteousness. For the justification of the sinner (3:27-28; 4:5) has its exclusive source in God's righteousness (= his faithfulness as the mark of his integrity). It can only be appropriated by faith and therefore excludes every human effort. It is dispensed "without works prescribed by the law" (3:28). Indeed, the climax of the argument of 1:18—4:25 is—as Luther saw so clearly—*sola fide*, "by faith alone." That faith, then, constitutes the unity of the church.

The third feature of the letter deals with the apocalyptic dimension of Paul's apostolic mandate (see above). Once the discussion of the sociological unity of Jew and Greek within the church is completed in terms of Paul's prophetic pronouncements (1:18—4:25), the *apocalyptic* dimension of his apostolic thought dominates the discussion in chapters 5–8.

Prophetic and apocalyptic categories now become intertwined. Once we see that the argument moves to another and new level in chapters 5–8, it becomes clear that the sociological issue of unity within the church is taken up into a cosmic-futurist framework. The intramural discussion about life within the walls of the church is then displaced by an extramural concern—the relation of the church to the power structures that rule the world; the alliance of the hostile powers of sin, death, the law, and the flesh. In other words, the issue of the power of sin that rules the world and threatens the church now receives an even more radical focus. It becomes, in chapters 5–8, the issue of the struggle between the apocalyptic powers of life and death.

So when we compare 1:18–4:25 with 5:1–8:39, we notice that the concerns of the church with its internal problems are now transcended, so that the relation of the church to the world outside the church comes into view. It is as if the windows of the church suddenly open themselves to the problems of the world.

The location of the church in the midst of a hostile world means struggle and suffering. However, the struggle of the church is not in vain; it lives in the hope of the ultimate triumph of God over the powers that poison his world (8:21)—a hope that is grounded in the gift of the Spirit, "the firstfruits" of God's coming glory (8:23).

Therefore, Paul's prophetic and apocalyptic conceptualities supplement each other. Indeed, the unity of the church (1:18–4:25) is not only the necessary prerequisite for its participation in God's coming triumph, but it also signifies the church's function as a beacon that signals the promise of the world's redemption.

The final feature to be discussed here deals with the meaning of "faith" (*pistis*) and its relation to "the Spirit" (*pneuma*). It is interesting to observe how complicated the relation between these terms is in Romans. The vocabulary of "Spirit" displaces that of "faith" in chapters 6–8, whereas to the contrary "faith," not "Spirit," occupies an exclusive role in chapters 1–5 (in chapter 4 alone the noun "faith" occurs ten times and the verb "to believe" occurs six times!).

Before the relation of Spirit and faith can be dealt with, we must first of all clarify the meaning of "faith" for Paul. Faith is essentially the human response to God's faithfulness in Christ. In other words, it means primarily trust in God's trustworthiness, manifested in his gift of righteousness. This definition of faith is most succinctly stated in 2 Corinthians 1:18-20: "As surely as God is faithful, our word to you has not been 'Yes and No.' For the Son of God, Jesus Christ, whom we proclaimed among you, was not 'Yes and No,' but in him it is always 'Yes.' For in him every one of God's promises is a 'Yes.' For this reason it is through him that we say the 'Amen' to the glory of God." In other words, faith is saying "Yes" to God's Yes in Christ. Therefore, it is not an intellectual assent to a proposition, but rather trust in God, "hearing" the gospel as an act of obedience (Rom. 1:5). Indeed, faith is not a human accomplishment or "work," but rather the grateful acknowledgment of being embraced by the Yes of God's grace toward us.

Paul uses the terminology of faith to proclaim our total dependence on God's grace, and thus functions as his primary tool in his anti-Jewish polemic, because the Jew believes that the law and the works it prescribes guarantee his salvation. However, we must be aware that the very context in which Paul uses faith in opposition to "boasting in the works of the law" (3:27) threatens to give faith a static connotation, as if faith signifies all that is necessary for our salvation.

The terminology of "faith" is unable to express sufficiently the ethical implications of the gospel. And so we notice that with the exception of Galatians 5:6 ("faith working through love"), Paul never uses "faith" in conjunction with the moral demands of the gospel.

For this reason Paul employs the terminology of "the Spirit" to complement the reality of faith in two aspects: First, since "the Spirit" is God's power in Christ, which pushes the believer into the future horizon of God's coming glory, it conveys *the dynamic character* of Christian life as a life of pilgrimage. Second, it denotes as well *the ethical dimension* of Christian life. In this context, Paul uses military metaphors to indicate the struggle of the Spirit against the flesh (8:12; cf. especially Galatians 5:17: "What the flesh desires is opposed to the Spirit, and what the Spirit desires is opposed to the flesh; for these are opposed to each other" [*antikeitai*]). Indeed, the Spirit is God's power, the equipment which enables believers to do battle with "the flesh" that rules this evil world. Accordingly, the Spirit is never separated from its activity in the human body.

So according to Paul, "faith" refers to the ground of our new relation to God, whereas "the Spirit" indicates that Christian life is a life *in via* (being under way). The life of pilgrimage, which moves us toward the future of God's final triumph, is made necessary because of the ongoing battle between "the Spirit" and the powers of sin, death, the flesh, and the law, by the ongoing threat of the world's powers that attempt to destroy the church.

Conclusion

IN THE PERSPECTIVE OF ROMANS, GOD'S FAITHFULNESS, WHICH HE has demonstrated to us in the death and resurrection of Christ, does not permit us to become complacent or self-assured, as if we have already obtained the fullness of salvation. We are forbidden to claim this, because God's own faithfulness will not come to a complete rest and fulfillment until the redemption of his whole suffering world is realized at the time of his coming triumph over the power of death and over everything in creation that resists his will. As Pascal said, "Jesus will be in agony until the end of the world. One should not sleep during that time."[1]

[1]Blaise Pascal, "Le Mystère de Jésus," *Pensées sur la Religion et sur quelques autres sujets*, 2nd ed. (Paris: Delmas, 1952) 334–37.

CHAPTER 6

The Pastoral Epistles

When we move from the authentic letters of Paul to letters written under his name, we must keep in mind that the period in which the Pastoral Epistles and the letter to the Ephesians were written was the second half of the first century A.D., the "era of the New Testament Pseudepigraphy."[1] K. M. Fischer, a prominent New Testament scholar, bases this judgment on the fact that between the time of the Pauline letters and the end of the first century, no early Christian writing carries the name of its true author. Rather, apostolic names are used as pseudonyms.

This judgment certainly applies to the Pastoral Epistles, which are a collection of three letters written at the end of the first century A.D. and never circulated separately. They were ostensibly addressed to churches in Ephesus and Crete in order to assist church leaders in their task of preaching, guiding, and organizational planning.

The letters' pseudonymity is twofold: They are supposedly written by Paul to supposedly two of his most intimate coworkers, Timothy and Titus, who are located, respectively, in Ephesus and on the island of Crete.

Outline of the Pastoral Epistles

I. 1 Timothy
   A. Prescript, 1:1-2

---

[1]K. M. Fischer, "Anmerkungen zur Pseudepigraphie im Neuen Testament," *NTS* 23 (1977) 76.

The Portrait of Paul

THE LETTERS' CLAIM TO AUTHORITY IS BASED SOLELY ON THE APOS-tle Paul's authority. In other words, legitimate Christianity and the authoritative gospel are identified exclusively with the gospel of Paul. In contrast to Luke-Acts, there is no appeal to other apostolic leaders or to the Jerusalem authorities. Indeed, as we shall see in our discussion of the Book of Acts, it grounds the validity of the gospel for the Gentiles on the decision of the apostolic college in Jerusalem (15:1-29) and emphasizes the harmonious unity of the church and its common "devotion to the apostles' teaching and fellowship" (2:42).

The Pastor conveys to his churches the unique apostolic authority of Paul and wants to maintain the continuity of Paul's gospel amidst the discontinuities of a different era. He writes after Paul's death, when the apostle could no longer be present or his *viva vox* heard.

The twofold pseudonymity of the Pastor's letters serves an important purpose: False attribution to Paul guarantees the continuity of the apostolic tradition after the death of the apostle. In this context the fictive name of Paul is crucial, because it is Paul who gives these letters their authoritative stature. Indeed, just as in the authentic letters of Paul, the name of the sender in the prescript undergirds Paul's personal authority and establishes the authoritative claim of his letters, so the name of Paul functions likewise for the Pastor, a feature that is confirmed by the close similiarity of the Pastoral Epistles to the letters of Paul.

Moreover, whenever the historical Paul was forced to be absent from his churches, he would maintain contact with them by means of letters and/or coworkers. Thus, it was natural for his later interpreters to continue this practice after Paul's death. In this way pupils of Paul were able to transmit the authority of the apostle by means of letters written in his name.

The figure of Paul is inextricably bound up with the reputation of the apostle in the area of Asia Minor, where the Pastoral Epistles were written. Since they are addressed to churches that were directly or indirectly the fruit of Paul's missionary labor, their portrait of Paul is heavily influenced by the historical impact of the apostle. Indeed, the impact of both Paul's letters and his missionary work contributed to his exclusive authority. Therefore, while the author seems to have known those letters of Paul, which circulated in the regions of Asia Minor—especially Romans, 1 Corinthians, and Philippians, although it is unlikely that the author of the Pastoral Epistles knew the complete collection of Paul's letters— regional circulation of some of his letters must be distinguished from the latter collection of the total Pauline corpus.[2] Paul's portrait in the Pastoral Epistles is actually a composite of literary references, legends, stories, and anecdotes.

Indeed, we must remember that various traditions combined to create Paul's portrait in the post-apostolic period. "Paul's portrait is here the reflection of the way in which the tradition has formed it. The readers saw before them 'the whole Paul, as they imagined him' (Jülicher, *Einleitung*, 172), and that was not simply the historical Paul, but the Paul who spoke to a post-Pauline era. Although the Pastoral Epistles were not directly written by Paul, they indicate the way in which a later generation saw and revered Paul."[3]

Thus, the Pastoral Epistles demonstrate the considerable distance between the historical Paul and the Paul depicted in the Pastoral Epistles. This is confirmed by other features of Paul's portrait. In the first place, the Paul of the Pastoral Epistles has become such an established authority

---

[2]Cf. L. Mowry, "The Early Circulation of Paul's Letters," *JBL* 63 (1964) 73–86.
[3]K. H. Schelkle, *Das Neue Testament* (Kevelaer Rhineland: Butzon & Bercker, 1963) 83; cf. also N. Brox, *Die Pastoralbriefe* (RNT 7:2; Regensburg: Verlag F. Pustet, 1969) 74.

that a simple appeal to his words and admonitions suffices to silence all questions and arguments. The impact of the transmission of tradition in the post-Pauline period shows itself in that Paul has now become "the great Paul" whose reputation and missionary success everyone in the church must acknowledge. In fact, Paul has achieved such an exclusive status that he simply argues *from* his unquestionable apostolic authority to a submissive church, rather than being forced to argue *for* his authority against his detractors in his churches, as the historical Paul was compelled to do.

In the second place, the historical distance between the historical Paul and the Paul of the Pastoral Epistles manifests itself in another significant feature of these letters. Paul's polemic with the Torah and Judaism is no longer a live issue in the Pastoral Epistles. The confrontation with Judaism—so prominent in Paul's Letters, Luke-Acts, Mark, Matthew, and John—is a thing of the past and has ceased to be a concern for the Paul of the Pastoral Epistles. Indeed, the churches of the Pastoral Epistles are largely made up of Gentiles and are seemingly alienated from the Jewish roots of Christianity. In fact, the conflict of the historical Paul with Jewish opponents is here replaced by a Paul who must combat Jewish-Gnostic heretics within the church.

The characteristic feature of Paul's portrait in the Pastoral Epistles becomes clear when we compare them with Acts. Although the Pastoral Epistles and Acts both draw their portrait of Paul from various legends and narratives about Paul that circulated in Paul's missionary territories in Asia Minor and Greece, their use of Paul's letters differs radically. Whereas the Pastoral Epistles cite and allude to them extensively, Acts ignores them completely. Thus, although the Pastoral Epistles are, like Acts, dependent on traditions *about* Paul, they are, unlike Acts, also indebted to the thought *of* Paul. Accordingly, the exclusivity of Paul's authority in the Pastoral Epistles sharply contrasts with its portrayal in Acts, where Paul is denied apostolic status and where his message is harmonized with that of the Jerusalem apostles.

The Relation of the Pastor's Method to His Message

IMPORTANT DIFFERENCES SURFACE WHEN WE COMPARE THE PAStor's structure of argumentation (his *method*) and the material content of his thought (his *message*) with those of the Paul of the authentic letters.

First, a word about the *method* employed by the Paul of the Pastoral Epistles. The intricate and flexible manner in which the historical Paul integrates the coherence of his gospel with the various contingent situations of his missionary churches undergoes a profound change. Since the historical Paul does not sever the coherence of the gospel from its contingent applicability, their relationship never becomes a matter of casuistically imposing a fixed body of authoritative teaching on the situation at hand. Indeed, Paul's ability to interweave coherence and contingency in a flexible manner conforms to the dialogical character of his hermeneutic. Paul's rhetoric with its polemical and persuasive strategies shows the lively presence of his partners in the dialogue both when they demand clarification or when they radically oppose Paul. For instance, Paul is regularly engaged in defending his apostolic status against those who either dispute it altogether (2 Corinthians) or indict him for falsely claiming to have independent apostolic status (Galatians).

However, in the Pastoral Epistles the lively dialogical structure of Paul's argumentation has collapsed. Paul's exclusive authority and the undisputed validity of his teaching demonstrate how the tradition causes an increasing "depersonalization" and "dehistoricization" of the apostle so that a movement toward creating a legendary portrait of Paul is under way. Indeed, we observe here the beginning of an apostolic hagiography.

For instance, Ignatius portrays the apostles as a heavenly council that symbolically represents the order of the church: "Likewise, let all respect the deacons as Jesus Christ, even as the bishop is also a type of the Father, and the presbyters as the council of God and the college of apostles" (Trall. 3:1; cf. also Magn. 6:1; likewise, 1 Clement and Polycarp present the apostles as one undifferentiated unity [1 Clem. 42:1; 44:1; Polycarp, Phil. 9:1], whereas the apocryphal Acts of the Apostles describes them as fantastic miracle workers and global missionaries).

In the Pastoral Epistles, dehistoricization takes the form of presenting Paul basically as a static and dogmatic person, notwithstanding the personal features of Paul's portrait in 2 Timothy.

Paul is thus portrayed mainly as a figure who simply imposes doctrine and is engaged in monologue. The Pauline gospel has now become a "deposit of truth" ([*parathēkē*] 1 Tim. 6:20; 2 Tim. 1:14) and "sound doctrine" ([*hygiainousa didaskalia*] 1 Tim. 1:10; 2 Tim. 4:3).

Indeed, the Paul of the Pastoral Epistles does not take the theological claims of his opponents seriously, but rather vilifies and stereotypes them as empty hotheads and moral perverts (for instance, "men, depraved in mind and bereft of the truth" [1 Tim. 6:5]; "evil men and impostors" [2 Tim. 3:13]; "empty talkers and deceivers" [Tit. 1:10]).

Thus, the dialogical method of the historical Paul, that is, his method of interweaving coherence and contingency, is displaced in the Pastoral Epistles by a *bifurcation* of coherence and contingency, because the timeless, rigid, and abstract character of the coherence of the gospel is unable to relate itself properly to the challenges of the contingent situation. Moreover, the contingency of the situation is here frivolously misrepresented, caricatured, and not deemed worthy of serious rebuttal.

Now a word about *the message* of the Paul of the Pastoral Epistles. The bifurcation of coherence and contingency affects not only the author's method of argumentation, but also his presentation of Paul's message. Because the author intends to be faithful to Paul and to Paul alone as the "paradigm" and "prototype" of Christian truth (1 Tim. 1:16; cf. 2:7; 2 Tim. 1:11-12), references to Paul's terminology and conceptuality abound, along with frequent allusions to his letters.[4]

We must be aware of the great influence that the transmission of tradition exerts here. The inevitable historicity of language and of language patterns gives rise to considerable changes in the meaning of traditional words and concepts, which must now function within a very different theological and sociohistorical context.

Thus, the author's abundant use of Paul's terminology must not deceive us. The bifurcation of coherence and contingency produces a linguistic structure that petrifies Paul's dynamic coherent language and therefore relates itself only artificially to its contingent situation. In fact,

---

[4]Notice the frequent occurrence of Pauline terms such as the following: "faith" (*pistis*, 32 times); "in [the] faith" (*en pistei*, 1 Tim. 1:2, 4; 2:7, 15; 3:13; 4:12; 2 Tim. 1:13; Tit. 1:13; 3:15); "to believe/entrust" (*pisteuein*, 1 Tim. 1:11, 16; 3:16; 2 Tim. 1:12; Tit. 1:3; 3:8); "righteous/just" (*dikaios*, 1 Tim. 1:9; 2 Tim. 4:8; Tit. 1:8); "to justify/vindicate" (*dikaioun*, 1 Tim. 3:16; Tit. 3:7); "righteousness" (*dikaiosynē*, 1 Tim. 6:11; 2 Tim. 2:22; 3:16; 4:8; Tit. 3:5); "love" (*agapē*, 1 Tim. 2:15; 4:12; 5: 14; 6:11; 2 Tim. 1:7, 13; 2:22; 3:10; Tit. 2:2, 10); "to love" (*agapein*, 2 Tim. 4:8, 10); "beloved" (*agapētos*, 1 Tim. 6:2; 2 Tim. 1:2); "hope/to hope" (*elpis/elpizein*, 1 Tim. 1:1; 3:14; 4:10; 5:5; 6:17; Tit. 1:2; 2:13; 3:7); "to save" (*sōzein*, 1 Tim. 1:15; 2:4, 15; 4:16; 2 Tim. 1:9; 4:18; Tit. 3:5); "grace" (*charis*, 1 Tim. 1:2, 14; 6:21; 2 Tim. 1:2, 9; 2:1; 4:22; Tit. 1:4; 2:11; 3:7, 15); "peace" (*eirēnē*, 1 Tim. 1:2; 2 Tim. 1:2; 2:22; Tit. 1:4); "to urge/exhort" (*parakalein*, 1 Tim. 1:3; 2:1; 5:1; 6:2; 2 Tim. 4:2; Tit. 1:9; 2:6, 15); cf. also "exhortation" (*paraklēsis*, 1 Tim. 4:13). To this list we may add the close similarity of the letter openings and closings to those of Paul.

Paul's concepts have now become sacrosanct and "holy" words to which the tradition has given a fixed and frozen meaning, becoming "holy tradition." And so they have lost their dynamic interrelation with the particular contingent situation, in and for which they originally functioned.

Moreover, the author's appeal to the specificity of Paul's gospel is deflected by a worldview that differs sharply from that of Paul's time. The author is much more at home in the atmosphere of a Hellenistic-Christian conceptuality and piety, which is foreign to Paul's description of the redemptive event: It centers on a Christology of "appearance" (*epiphaneia*, 1 Tim. 6:14; 2 Tim. 1:10; 4:1, 8)[5] and on a characterization of either God or Christ as "Savior" (*soter*, 2 Tim. 1:10; Tit. 3:4–6).

In addition, the piety of the Pastoral Epistles is characterized by non-Pauline terms, such as "piety"/"godliness" (*eusebeia*, 1 Tim. 2:2; 3:16, 4:7-8; 5:6, 6:3, 11; 2 Tim. 3:5; Tit. 1:1); "the teaching," "doctrine" (*didaskalia*, 1 Tim. 4:6; 6:3); "sound doctrine" (*hygiainousa didaskalia*, 1 Tim. 1:10; 2 Tim. 4:3; Tit. 1:9; 2:1); and "the sound words" (*hygiainontes logoi*, 1 Tim. 6:3; 2 Tim. 1:13).

In other words, when the author blends central concepts of the "original" Paul with his own Hellenistic conceptuality, they lose their original meaning and now become threadbare language. For instance, "righteousness" (*dikaiosyne*) has—except in 2 Tim. 4:8—no longer its Pauline meaning of God's redemptive intervention in Christ, but instead signifies a pragmatic moral injunction (cf. "aim at righteousness" [1 Tim. 6:11; 2 Tim. 2:22]); "all scripture . . . is profitable . . . for training (*pros paideian*) in righteousness" (2 Tim. 3:16; cf. also Tit. 3:5). In fact, the original meaning of Paul's use of the verb "to justify" (*dikaioun*) is only present in texts where the author incorporates early Christian liturgical traditions in his letters (1 Tim. 3:16; Tit. 3:7). Moreover, Paul's correlation of the noun "righteousness," and the verb "to justify" (*dikaio* – terminology), with "faith" (*pistis*), "the law" (*nomos*), and "works" (*erga*) is either absent or has a quite different connotation:

> Frequently "faith" (*pistis*) continues to indicate the maintenance of the faith (e.g., I 1:5) as well as the rule of faith (I 3:9; 6:10; II 4:7), so that often the formula "in faith" (*en pistei*) appears (I 1:2; 2:7). Indeed, in parallel with this sense of "faith" (*pistis*) stands

---

[5]The noun and the verb "to appear" (*epiphaneia* and *epiphanesthai*, respectively) can also refer to God (Tit. 2:11, 3:4) or to both God and Christ (Tit. 2:13).

"sound doctrine" (*kalē didaskalia*) (I 4:6). This rationalistic ethical description of Christian existence and the Christian obligation corresponds to the use of the plural "good works" (*erga agatha*; as in Eph. 2:10; I 2:10; Tit. 2:14.[6]

With the exception of the liturgical piece of Titus 3:4-7, which contrasts "works done by us in righteousness" (verse 5) with justification by grace (verse 7), the frequent occurrence of "works" (*erga*) in the Pastoral Epistles is always conjoined with the adjectives "good" (*kala* or *agatha*, 1 Tim. 2:10; 3:1; 5:10, 22; 6:18; 2 Tim. 1:9; 2:21; 3:17; 4:5, 14, 18; Tit. 1:16; 2:7, 14; 3:1, 8, 14). Furthermore, "the infrequent use of *en Christo*, which is almost wholly restricted to a combination with abstract nouns in a way that is never encountered in Paul,"[7] coupled with the virtual omission of terms like "body" (*sōma*) and Spirit (*pneuma*; cf. 2 Tim. 1:14 and Tit. 3:5), shows clearly the distance between the Paul of history and the Paul of the Pastoral Epistles.

The Theological Identity of the Pastoral Epistles

ALTHOUGH WE MUST ACKNOWLEDGE THE SHORTCOMINGS OF the Pastoral Epistles in transmitting the historical message of Paul, we should also appreciate the attempt of its author to make Paul a living voice for the so different situation of his time. Since the author is not interested in an archaeological search for the "original" Paul, he understands faithfulness to Paul's gospel to consist in adapting that gospel to the new situation of his churches so that it can be a word on target for them. Thus, he does not consider faithfulness to Paul to consist in a literal transposition of Paul's thought, but rather as a search for innovative strategies that permit Paul to speak in a fresh manner. What to many of us seems to be "a fall from the true Paul" is, for the Pastor, an appropriate reinterpretation and reinstatement of Paul's gospel.

This reinterpreted and relevant Paul must safeguard the continuity of the true Pauline gospel in the church by addressing two specific dangers that threaten its life: there is not only a danger from *within*, that is, inner-ecclesial dissension, but also a perilous danger from *without*, that is, so-

---

[6]W. G. Kümmel, *Introduction to the New Testament*, trans. H. C. Kee (revised edition; Nashville: Abingdon Press, 1975) 383.
[7]Ibid., p. 373.

cioeconomic pressures and political oppression by Roman society and state. The danger from without is brought about by the new situation of the church in history. For the church cannot any longer maintain its sectarian character, and remain a contra-society in the Pauline sense—that is, a community that is basically opposed to the world. Since history seems to have an ongoing and continuing flow, it is perceived in a way that differs from Paul's perception. For instance, Paul's conviction, "The appointed time has grown very short" (1 Cor. 7:29), is no longer a live issue for the church of the Pastoral Epistles, because the church now has an urgent need to secure a stable position within the structures of the ongoing world of Roman society.

Thus, it must face the issue of how to be "*in mundo, sed non mundi*"—that is, how to adapt itself to its new situation in the world. Although the Pastor remains committed to the faith of Paul and early Christianity, that the eschatological judgment and glory of God are to be expected (1 Tim. 6:14-15; 2 Tim. 4:8; Tit. 2:13), his adoption of a Christology that emphasizes a completed presence of salvation in Christ (cf. his *epiphaneia* Christology), coupled with his heavy emphasis on matters of ecclesial order and administration (1 Tim. 2:1-12; Tit. 1:5—2:10), show his fading interest in the imminent coming of the end time. Indeed, the author actually advocates cautious accommodation to the secular world of the Roman Empire; prayers and intercessions are to be made "for kings and all who are in high positions, so that we may lead a quiet and peaceable life in all godliness and dignity" (1 Tim. 2:1-2).

Moreover, he insists that a bishop must "be well thought of by outsiders" (1 Tim. 3:7), while young widows should "marry, bear children, manage their households, so as to give the adversary no occasion to revile us" (1 Tim. 5:14, cf. Tit. 2:5, 8). Thus, the author hopes that the church, by conforming to the moral customs of Roman society, may lead "a quiet and peaceable life" (1 Tim. 2:2) and gain a good report from "outsiders" (1 Tim. 3:7) and "opponents" alike (Tit. 2:8).

The author's second concern, that is, about the danger from within is directly related to the danger from without. It is the result of heretical inroads within the church that threaten its nonoffensive character by their antisocial behavior. The confrontation with heresy preoccupies the author to such an extent that it would be appropriate to call the Pastoral Epistles polemical antiheretical letters. In fact, heretics are "the enemy" (1 Tim. 5:14) in a double sense: They not only pervert the orthodoxy of the church, but are also liable to evoke the hostile attitude of Roman society against persons who upset its civil and moral order.

It is conspicuous how differently Paul and the Pastor define Christian existence. Conzelmann observes: "This ideal of a peaceful life differs greatly from Paul's understanding of existence, which reflects the many conflicts of his life; one need only compare this passage (1 Tim. 2:2) with the description which the apostle gives in 2 Cor. 11:23-33 of his life's difficulties and dangers. Paul lives in the tension between this world and God's world: he joyfully affirmed (in 2 Cor. 6:4-10) the suffering of this existence as part of citizenship in the other kingdom—the Pastor wishes to become part of the world."[8] And Brox comments: "We must notice here, in contrast to the Revelation of John, the beginning of Christianity's accommodation to the world."[9]

Although such observations are correct, they do not sufficiently appreciate the sociocultural situation that prompts the theological response of the author. In fact, Conzelmann tempers his earlier remarks when he writes later in his commentary: "For an historical understanding it is not enough simply to confront this ethical idea [of the Pastoral Epistles] with the ethics of Jesus or Paul. It is necessary to consider the changed situation of the church and to interpret the Pastoral Epistles together with contemporary writings (*Luke* and the *Apostolic Fathers*), in the context of a changing conceptual structure—change had to follow the reorientation toward a longer duration of life in the world."[10]

Indeed, the author's conception of what life in an ongoing world demands is directly related to his response to the danger from within. For the church's desire for peace and stability in its relation to the world matches its desire to eradicate heretical thought and practice within the church. The author fears that if the heretical opposition with its pro-feminist, emancipatory asocial behavior and deviant thought prevails,[11] the Roman authorities and society-at-large will threaten the very survival of the church. Indeed, the author's opposition to heresy is motivated not only by the limits that "Paul's" gospel draws between the church and the world—by an "over-the-shoulder" look at the reaction of Roman society—but especially by the limits that his gospel draws between "orthodoxy" and "heresy." As Brox correctly observes: "Notwithstanding

---

[8]Martin Dibelius & Hans Conzelmann, *The Pastoral Epistles*, trans. P. Buttolph & A. Yarbro (Hermeneia; Philadelphia: Fortress Press, 1972) 39.
[9]Norbert Brox, *Die Pastoralbriefe* (see n. 3 above), p.124.
[10]Dibelius & Conzelmann, *The Pastoral Epistles*, pp.40-41.
[11]Cf. D. R. MacDonald, *The Legend and the Apostle: The Battle for Paul in Story and Canon* (Philadelphia: Westminster, 1983).

the overlap with a pragmatic, 'opportune' mentality, the distinctive character of the Pastoral Epistles is maintained in two ways: in the vitality and motivation which is grounded in the preaching of Christ and [in] the boundaries which this understanding of faith (in 2 Tim.) draws in a situation of persecution, since the Pastoral Epistles accomplish and accept a reduction to what is most essential to the Christian confession."[12]

However, the author's method of dealing with his opponents makes it difficult to gain an intelligible profile of the heretics. His desire to *contemporize* Paul's authority for his churches directly contradicts Paul's own method of dealing with heretical movements because, as we saw above, the delicate balance in Paul between coherence and contingency is here displaced by a fixed coherent structure that has no direct relation to the contingent crisis situation which the Pastoral Epistles must face. Instead, the coherence of the gospel functions here to drown the heretical opposition into a sea of rhetorical attacks, and thus obfuscates its real nature. The author demands that church officials refrain from any contact with heretics because discussions with them are deemed to be not only dangerous, but even superfluous: "Avoid disputing about words (*logomachein*), which does no good, but only ruins the hearers" (2 Tim. 2:14; cf. also 1 Tim. 6:20; 2 Tim. 2:33; Tit. 3:9). Instead, the proper way of dealing with heretics is either "to correct the opponents" (2 Tim. 2:24) or "to have nothing to do with profane myths and old wives' tales" (1 Tim. 4:7). "One can describe the situation in this way: The Pastoral Epistles actually do not combat the heresy, but rather the heretics."[13] The fiction of Pauline authorship becomes very clear here: "Paul" not only warns against the influx of present heresies in the church (1 Tim. 1:3, 19-20; 6:20; 2 Tim. 2:16; 3:8; Tit. 1:10; 3:9), but also predicts these same heresies for the future end time (1 Tim. 4:1-5; 2 Tim. 3:1f., 13; 4:3f.). Thus, Paul's prediction of *future* heresies and his active struggle with *present* heresies have identical heresies in mind. Indeed, they represent the author's attempt to bridge the gulf that separates the time of the historical Paul from that of his Paul.

Conclusion

Two observations by Brox help us to appreciate more adequately the Pastor's adaptation of Paul: "The Pastoral Epistles can only

---

[12]Brox, *Die Pastoralbriefe*, p.125.
[13]V. Hasler, *Die Briefe an Timotheus und Titus*, 68; quoted in Brox, ibid. p. 39.

be understood and correctly appraised within their historical-theological context if one pays attention to the enormous structural change (*Struk-turwandel*) which the church experienced, with which it had to come to terms and which through its effort it had to transmit again to new generations. A new orientation of the 'old' became a necessity. It was here attempted and solved by allowing 'Paul' to speak in 'letters' to the contemporary church."[14] And again: "And indeed when one allowed 'Paul' to speak, it was done without simply repeating him. Rather one permitted him to speak in a way which was appropriate to the changed situation. It should be noted that this interpretation of Paul was not a conscious effort. However, precisely this interpretation of Paul understood Paul and his theology essentially better than a mere historicizing treatment of the apostle, which is sometimes the reason for the disparaging manner in which the Pastoral Epistles and their theology are treated by exegetes."[15]

We conclude, then, that in terms of the situation the author had to deal with, he offers us an impressive portrait of Paul. His Paul not only combats present heresies (1 Tim. 1:19-20; 2 Tim. 2:17) and prophesies heresies to come in the end time (1 Tim. 4:1-5), but he also gives orders and exhortations to his coworkers about how to conduct worship and organize the life of the church. Moreover, Paul is the *sole* apostle, a person who enjoys indisputable authority and whose gospel is the sole norm of Christian truth.

Finally, Paul's words are all the more binding because the author casts them in the form of a farewell address—as the last will and testament of the apostle who has suffered for the sake of the gospel and who now, from his death-cell, bids his successors to suffer likewise for the truth of the gospel (2 Tim. 1:8; 2:3; 4:5, 17) and to conserve "the deposit" of faith (*parathēkē*, 1 Tim. 6:20; 2 Tim. 1:12, 14) unblemished. In this manner, "Paul" ensures the continuity of the tradition amidst the discontinuities of history, so that later generations can render his orthodox gospel faithfully.

Above all, although we may disparage the Pastor's treatment of Paul and especially his attempt to turn "the difficult theological Paul" of the

---

[14]N. Brox, "Amt, Kirche und Theologie in der nachapostolischen Epoche: die Pastoralbriefe," in *Gestalt und Anspruch des Neuen Testaments*, ed. J. Schreiner (Würzburg: Echter-Verlag, 1969) 132.
[15]Ibid., p. 123.

letters into "a simple pastoral Paul," who can easily be appropriated, we should also recognize the author's insistence on the necessary bond between a Christian's word and deed. This is a very relevant word for our time, when all too frequently theological rhetoric is deemed more important than personal integrity and moral honesty. It may well be that at the Last Judgment theological ingenuity will count for nothing compared to the ethical truthfulness the Pastor demands of us.

CHAPTER 7

The Letter to the Ephesians

LIKE THE PASTORAL EPISTLES, EPHESIANS CLAIMS TO BE A LETTER of Paul. It is addressed to the church at Ephesus where, according to Acts 19, Paul had done missionary work for more than three years. However, Ephesians itself indicates that Paul was not directly responsible for founding the church there (1:15; 3:2).

The close literary dependence of Ephesians on Colossians is well established in scholarship: "The kinship of Ephesians with Colossians is undoubtedly far greater than the kinship of any other letter of Paul with the rest of the Pauline corpus: about a third of the words in Colossians are found again in Ephesians. Only brief portions of Ephesians (for instance, 2:6-9; 4:5-13; 5:29-33) have no verbal parallels in Colossians."[1]

There are, in fact, many theological similarities between the two letters. Nevertheless, Ephesians is not slavishly dependent on its predecessor, but develops its own literary style and theological focus. To be sure, the structure of the two letters is much the same; they conform closely to the composition of Paul's letters in that the ethical sections are placed after the theological expositions (Col. 1–2, 3–4; Eph. 1–3, 4–6). However, the purpose and theological perspective of Colossians and Ephesians show remarkable differences. Whereas Colossians is a personal and contingent letter that addresses particular problems in the churches of the Lycus Valley (Western Asia Minor) and combats a specific heretical opposition, Ephesians, to the contrary, lacks any such personal

---

[1]Kümmel, *Introduction*, pp.358–59.

and specific features. It is instead an encyclical letter that addresses a group of churches, probably located in Asia Minor, to instruct them in basic matters of theology and ethics.

The differences between Colossians and Ephesians resemble in many ways the differences between Paul's letters to the Galatians and to the Romans. Both Colossians and Galatians are marked by a close interrelation between coherent theological exposition and contingent situations, whereas in both Ephesians and Romans, the coherent theological exposition is so dominant that its relation to the contingent, situational problems of the churches addressed is either completely absent (Ephesians) or difficult to determine (Romans). Therefore, it is not surprising when scholars call Romans "a compendium of Christian doctrine" (Melanchthon; see above) and when they characterize Ephesians as "the quintessence of Paulinism."[2]

The Outline of the Letter

    I. Prescript, 1:1-2

    II. Part I—Exposition, 1:3—3:21 (The mystery of God's plan of salvation and the call of the Gentiles into the church)

        A. Praise to God for his plan of salvation, 1:3-14

        B. Intercession for the Gentiles, 1:15-23

        C. The nature of salvation, 2:1—3:13

        D. Intercession and Doxology, 3:14-21

    III. Part II—Exhortation, 4:1—6:20 (A lifestyle in conformity to the call of the gospel)

        A. The unity of the church as the basis and norm of the Christian life, 4:1-16

        B. Warning against a pagan lifestyle, 4:17-24

        C. Specific warnings, 4:25—5:20

        D. Household codes, 5:21—6:9

        E. The armor of God, 6:10-20

        F. Conclusion, 6:21-24

---

[2]F. F. Bruce, *Paul: Apostle of the Heart Set Free* (Grand Rapids, Mich.: Eerdmans, 1977) 424.

The Purpose of the Letter

EPHESIANS WAS WRITTEN AFTER PAUL'S DEATH TO CHURCHES IN the area of Paul's mission in Asia Minor. It aims to strengthen the churches and to exhort them to remain faithful to their apostle Paul, who is now no longer with to them. Indeed, what were teachers faithful to Paul's gospel to do? In Paul's day there had been the possibility of immediate access to Paul and to his apostolic authority and intervention. But now a more difficult situation had arisen.

Whereas in Paul's day there existed a *spatial distance* (geographical) between Paul and his churches, which could be bridged by his letters or his coworkers serving as substitutes for his personal presence, now a more difficult distance had to be bridged—a *temporal distance* and gap between the time of Paul's personal missionary activity and the period after his death in the late first century A.D. How could this distance be bridged? How was the apostle to speak again to his churches in the post-apostolic situation? Thus, like the author of the Pastoral Epistles, the author of Ephesians faces the problem of how the apostolic Pauline tradition is to be re-presented and reactualized in a new contingent situation after the apostle's death. The author—a pupil of Paul—solves the problem by speaking in the name of Paul to his churches, that is, by interpreting the Pauline tradition in terms of the concerns and problems of his own time and situation. In this manner the author not only transmits what he believes to be the gospel of Paul, but also sketches an impressive portrait of the apostle.

The Gospel of Paul according to Ephesians

THE AUTHOR CONSTRUCTS A THEOLOGY OF PAUL THAT CENTERS on "the mystery of Christ" (3:3-4; 6:15), by which he means the unity of Jew and Gentile in the one body of Christ (2:14-22; 3:6; 4:15-16). We discern here the ecclesiological focus of Ephesians. Whereas the author of Colossians defines the mystery always as Christ (1:26, 27; 2:2; cf. 4:3), the author of Ephesians interprets the mystery in a different manner—in terms of the universal church (2:19; cf. 2:11-21).

Indeed, this ecclesiological concern dominates the letter throughout. The eulogy at the beginning of the letter (1:3-14) praises the God who "chose us in Christ before the foundation of the world to be holy and blameless before him in love" and determined "as a plan for the fullness of time, to gather up all things in him (Christ), things in heaven and things on earth" (1:4, 10). The God who "is able to accomplish abundantly far more than all we can ask or imagine" (3:20) has now "made him (Christ) the head over all things for the church, which is his body, the fullness of him who fills all in all" (1:22-23). Moreover, the plan of God, which climaxes in the unity of Jew and Gentile in the one "household of God" (2:19; cf. 2:11-21) has a cosmic range. For it is through the church that "the wisdom of God in its rich variety might now be made known to the rulers and authorities in the heavenly places" (3:10; cf. 1:10). The ecclesiological focus of the author even leads him to conjoin Christ and the church—a symbiosis that resembles the joining of husband and wife to "become one flesh" (5:31). And yet the mystical union of Christ and the church does not lead the author to a complete fusion between the two. He never forgets that "the husband is the head of the wife just as Christ is the head of the church" (5:23; cf. also 1:22; 4:15).

However, we must notice that the author's ecclesiological, speculative, and wisdom-like ruminations have a pragmatic purpose because his ecclesiological and cosmic reflections serve a practical moral purpose— the upbuilding of the church. This emphasis pervades not only the section of the letter that is exclusively devoted to ethics (4:1—6:9), but rather permeates the letter as a whole (1:4, 12, 19; 2:1, 8, 10; 3:17-19). For instance, the author significantly elaborates the household codes that he derives from Colossians (5:2-6, 9; cf. Col. 3:18—4:1) and "Christianizes" them much more extensively than Colossians. Indeed, his admonitions are not restricted to wives and husbands as in Colossians (cf. Col. 3:18-19), but also address the "masters" of slaves (cf. Col. 4:1; Eph. 5:22-33; 6:9). Moreover, the dualistic-apocalyptic texture of the concluding section of the letter (6:10-18), with its imagery of the armor of God and "the cosmic powers of this present darkness" (6:10, 12) indicates the practical focus of the author's ecclesiology when he urges Christians to oppose in their daily life the demonic powers that rule this world.

The Author's Portrait of Paul

In accordance with the author's ecclesiological focus, he portrays Paul as the *ecclesial* apostle who is not only a Catholic liturgist, but also an ethical teacher. In addition, he celebrates Paul as the mystagogue whose insight into the mystery of God's revelation surpasses that of all other apostles and prophets (3:4). Paul is uniquely appointed to disclose this mystery, which—as we have seen—focuses on the union of Gentiles and Jews into the one body of Christ (3:1-8; cf. also 2:1-22).

The exalted status of the apostle Paul in Ephesians is remarkable. Besides being the unique apostle, he is also the martyr who not only suffers (3:13) for the sake of the gospel, but also is imprisoned for it (3:1; 4:1; 6:20)—a point that the author underscores dramatically at the conclusion of the letter: "Pray also for me, so that when I speak, a message may be given to me to make known with boldness the mystery of the gospel, for which I am an ambassador in chains" (6:19-20; cf. also Col. 4:18, "Remember my chains.").

The Worldview of the Letter

IN ORDER TO UNDERSTAND EPHESIANS PROPERLY, WE MUST BE AWARE that the author's theology is delineated in terms of the worldview of his audience. The author is no longer committed to the temporal-eschatological framework of the letters of Paul. That framework was dominated by the tension of the "already-not yet"—a theology determined by the basic structure of an apocalyptic, Jewish worldview, and by a Christology characterized by the anticipation of the coming glory of God. In other words, Christ's death and resurrection meant for Paul "the firstfruits" (Rom. 8:23; 1 Cor. 15:20) that inaugurate the full harvest of God's cosmic future reign.

However, the author of Ephesians lives in a time when Paul's imminent expectation of God's coming final glory is no longer the object of fervent hope. Instead, he must convey Paul's gospel within the framework of a Hellenistic cosmology.

It is a worldview in which Paul's *temporal-horizontal* frame of "now and then" is displaced by a *spatial-vertical* conception of "up and down." This vertical conception expresses a cosmology of heavenly spheres, dominated by layers of supernatural powers that in a hierarchical way reign over the heaven and earth. This cosmology explains the rich, cosmic-power language of Ephesians (and also of Colossians)—a language that is almost completely absent in Paul's letters: "the heavenly places" (1:20; 3:10); "the ruler of the power of the air" (2:2); "the aeon of this world" (2:2); "[Christ] seated him at his [God's] right hand in the heavenly places, far above all rule and authority and power and dominion" (1:20-21); "the cosmic powers of this present darkness, the spiritual forces of evil in the heavenly places" (6:12). Although within the framework of this cosmology, salvation is defined as the knowledge of how to escape these spheres of the evil powers that rule this world in order to ascend to God's heavenly places, Ephesians does not celebrate a dualistic-escapist concept of salvation. Rather, it celebrates Christ as our peace because he has accomplished a cosmic reconciliation (2:13–22) and has raised us up with himself to the heavenly places (2:6). Thus, "the heavenly church" is able to announce on earth to the "heavenly powers" that they have been destroyed in Christ (3:10), "so that he [Christ] might fill all things" (4:10).

Conclusion

HOW, THEN, SHALL WE APPROPRIATE THE THEOLOGY OF EPHESIANS?

Paul's portrait in the letter conforms to its vision of the church as the *una sancta catholica et apostolica ecclesia.* Paul is here remembered by his pupil (the author of Ephesians) after his death as a figure whose authority and status have increased enormously over time. He is now nostalgically transmitted to the churches of Asia Minor as the apostle of sacred memory who has single-handedly converted the Gentiles to the church.

Ephesians transmits Paul's theology in a liturgical style and with a luxuriant overflow of language, which expresses its doxological texture. The letter suggests, as it were, a scenario of worship in a Greek Orthodox cathedral, dominated by a picture of a giant *Christus Rex* behind the altar.

Indeed, while songs of praise are offered and the incense thickens the air of the sanctuary, we watch the *ikonostasis* (the opening of the gates of the altar) at the moment of the eucharist. The opening of the doors of the altar intimates that at this moment the church becomes united with the heavenly regions where the risen Christ dwells at the right hand of the Father, so that the church's sanctuary becomes fused with heaven's glory. Indeed, the portrait of Paul of the marketplace—the historical Paul, God's lawyer against the idolatry of the nations—has here been transposed into Paul the liturgist, celebrating the glory of God in his church. And the focus of this celebration is Christ, who rules over all powers and authorities in heaven and on earth while the church—his body—utters its joyful praise to the God who has made the church Christ's extension on earth (cf. also 6:20).

Ephesians, with its cosmic-universal ecclesiology, its celebration of "the immeasurable greatness of his [God's] power" (1:19) and its theme of the reconciliation of Jew and Gentile (2:11-21), has an extraordinary appeal to our ecumenical age (cf. especially 4:1-6). However, we must not forget that the very feature that appeals to us so strongly disqualifies the letter in some ways as a faithful rendering of Paul's thought. Its encyclical character demonstrates that the most crucial aspect of Paul's way of doing theology—that is, the interplay between coherence and contingency—is here virtually ignored. The author of Ephesians sacrifices the *particularity* of Paul's theology for the sake of a catholic *universalism*, which enables him to transmit Paul's doctrinal gospel smoothly to every subsequent historical epoch. Therefore, the very feature of Ephesians that is so attractive to us— its non-situational, universal appeal—is exactly the feature that betrays its non-Pauline character.

Moreover, although the concept of the church is as well a central part of Paul's theology, ecclesiology has quite a different face in Ephesians. Here the universality of the apostolic-catholic church subordinates Paul's eschatology to his ecclesiology and displaces this eschatology with the concept of the church as a "divine commonwealth."[3] This is an important issue. For whenever eschatology and Christology are conflated, as in Ephesians, the concept of the church is inflated and its identification with the future eschatological kingdom becomes a real danger.

This raises the question of whether we can really surrender Paul's eschatological vision and its ethic of solidarity with all of God's creation. Once the notion of the church as a proleptic reality is displaced by an exclusive focus on the church as the mystical body of Christ in which all God's promises find their fulfillment, we adopt a concept of the church that celebrates its own salvation so exclusively that it disregards the plight of an unredeemed world.

Notwithstanding these reservations, we cannot but admire the creative and imaginative power of this letter. The author is aware of the need to reformulate Paul's gospel for the needs of his own time. And it is exactly this awareness that makes him true to Paul's own way of doing theology— that is, to translate the gospel in such a way that it becomes a word on target for the time and situation at hand.

[3]C. H. Dodd, *The Meaning of Paul for Today* (New York: George H. Doran, 1920) 139.

CHAPTER 8

Jesus and Human Fulfillment

I DO NOT INTEND TO REHEARSE HERE THE MANY PROBLEMS INHER-
ent in the search for the historical Jesus. That has been done masterfully
by Albert Schweitzer in *The Quest of the Historical Jesus*, which appeared
originally in 1906 under the title *Von Reimarus zu Wrede: Eine Geschichte
der Leben-Jesu-Forschung* and was translated into English in 1910. Nor will
I trace the developments since Schweitzer, that is, the emergence of the
new quest of the historical Jesus and the reactions to it.[1] However, it will
become clear that I assume the basic thesis of the New Quest. The New
Quest emphasizes in reaction to kerygmatic theologians, such as Bultmann, the continuity between the kerygma of the post-Easter church and
the teachings of the historical Jesus. Thus, I find myself in disagreement
with Bultmann when he states that Jesus is the presupposition of New
Testament theology rather than its fundamental subject. In accordance
with my thematic approach to the New Testament, I will restrict myself
to one hermeneutical aspect of the life of Jesus— his significance for our
Christian life today.

The Gospel Genre

WE MUST RECOGNIZE THAT THE GOSPEL WRITERS DID NOT INTEND
to produce a historical biography of the life of Jesus. The Gospels were
written from faith to faith, since they constitute reflections on the life of

---

[1] Albert Schweitzer, *The Quest of the Historical Jesus*, intro. J. M. Robinson (New
York: Macmillan, 1968); J. M. Robinson, *The New Quest.*

Jesus after the events of his death and resurrection. In other words, they are products of the faith of the early church, and it is clear that the individual authors of the Gospels incorporated many early Christian traditions and liturgical pieces into their Gospels.

This raises an important question: Why did the genre of the gospel become so important for the early church? Why was it considered necessary to write retrospective "lifes of Jesus" after Jesus had become the Christ, and the preaching of the crucified and risen Christ had become the central focus of the life and mission of the church?

Advocates of the neo-orthodox movement, a movement that arose in the wake of World War I, did not take this question seriously because for them, the whole New Testament preached only the Christ event. Thus, they espoused a so-called kerygmatic theology, which contrasts the attempts to sketch a historical life of Jesus with the preaching of the crucified and risen Christ. In the meantime, form criticism had demonstrated that the Gospels were the end products of oral transmission, originating in early Christian circles. Thus, kerygmatic theology was supported not only by the advances of form criticism, but also by the failure of the quest of the historical Jesus to sketch a coherent and authentic life of Jesus.

M. Kähler's book, *Der sogenannte historische Jesus und der geschichtliche biblische Christus* (*The So-Called Historical Jesus and the Historic Biblical Christ* [Philadelphia: Fortress, 1969]), published before the rise of the neo-orthodox movement, symbolizes this trend: "The real Christ is the Christ who is preached" ("Der wirkliche Christus ist der gepredigte Christus").[2]

However, the exclusive concentration on God's act in Jesus' crucifixion and resurrection by the kerygmatic theologians did not answer the question why the gospel genre emerged in early Christianity. They failed to realize that the production of gospel accounts became necessary in the period when apostolic eyewitnesses to Jesus' ministry had passed away. For with the deaths of the disciples and apostles of Jesus came the danger that the continuity between Jesus and the risen Christ would be lost. In other words, when the preaching of the gospel went out to the gentile mission field, the proclamation of Christ tended to become divorced from its moorings in the historical Jesus.

---

[2]Quote taken from W. G. Kümmel, *Das Neue Testament: Geschichte der Erforschung seiner Probleme* (Freiburg/München: Verlag Karl Alber, 1958) 284.

Thus, after the death of the apostles/disciples who had represented the bond between Jesus and the crucified, risen Christ, the Gospels filled a necessary need, for the question *whose* cross and resurrection demanded the faith of Christians had to be answered. Indeed, there was acute danger that the cross and resurrection would simply disintegrate into general symbolic ciphers without any precise content, for it was easy to confuse the death and resurrection of a "Christ" with the death-and-life ritual of the mystery religions or of the fertility cults. Thus, it became imperative to establish the continuity between the Christ of faith and the historical Jesus. The Gospels were produced in the first century A.D. for this explicit purpose. And it comes as no surprise that their retrospective reporting was motivated by the faith perspective of the early Christians. Therefore, a mixture of faith and historical reporting pervades the "lifes of Jesus" by the authors of the Gospels.

We must be aware that their intention in writing the Gospels remains a crucial issue for us. Thus, we can only applaud the attempt of the new quest of the historical Jesus to demonstrate the continuity between the historical Jesus and the Christ of faith.

The Significance of the Historical Jesus

WHAT, THEN, IS THE SIGNIFICANCE OF THE HISTORICAL JESUS FOR our faith today? What strikes us about Jesus and how is that which strikes us of existential importance for our lives? It has always been interesting to me that no theologian has ever produced a theology of Jesus. Is it not peculiar that amidst so many New Testament and Christian theologies, no theologian has ever ventured to write a theology of Jesus, whereas, presumably, all Christian theologies are based on the phenomenon of Jesus? It seems as if the initiator and subject of Christian theology is unable to be grasped theologically. That is indeed a puzzle. Part of the solution to that puzzle lies in the relation of the simple to the profound. Jesus' words and work seem so simple that they cannot be comprehended by using a complex theological conceptuality. Indeed, the puzzle becomes truly a mystery. For the mystery of Jesus' simplicity is located exactly in its profundity. The difficulty is that for us, the profound is always the complex, whereas the simple tends to be thoughtless and commonplace. However, in Jesus' case the situation is quite different. Here the simple and the profound coincide, and that constitutes a significant part of the mystery that is Jesus. For Jesus, the criterion of salvation or damnation is not some awesome theological construct, but rather the equally awesome yet simple word: "Let him who has ears to hear, hear."

The mystery of Jesus may be clarified for us when we compare the message of Jesus with that of Paul. The tools of Jesus are the parable, the story, and the metaphor. They are materials that derive from human experience and evoke it most directly. However, Paul is not a storyteller nor does he use the parable as a means of communication.

Although Paul uses and creates powerful metaphors and images, his extended metaphors usually fail (Rom. 11:17-24) or turn into allegorizations (Rom. 7:1-3; cf. Gal. 4:21-26). Paul is a man of the proposition, the argument, and the dialogue, not a man of the parable or the story. We must remember that the story unfolds, whereas the concept defines. The story is multidimensional, the concept singular. The story opens up horizons for imaginative participation, whereas the concept delineates a specific boundary for thought. Robert Funk says it well when discussing the nature of language in the context of Jesus' use of the parable:

> The parable brings into the foreground language as the medium of discovery over against sedimentation—language in which significations are preestablished. . . . All language is indirect or allusive. Speech never comes to rest in itself, as though there were nothing left to be said. . . . Rather language remains unfinished because signifying is always surpassed by the signified. Just as unspoken language, primordial discourse, precedes articulation, so it follows articulation: articulation is bounded by the silent word, from which it proceeds and to which it returns.[3]

Indeed, "Jesus speaks in the lowest abstractions that language is capable of—if it is to be language at all and not the fact itself."[4] "The parable stands thus at the frontier of language and mirrors without conceptualizing the kingdom of God."[5]

---

[3]Robert W. Funk, *Language, Hermeneutic and Word of God: The Problem of Language in the New Testament and Contemporary Theology* (New York: Harper & Row, 1966) 230.

[4]Alfred N. Whitehead, *Religion in the Making* (New York: Macmillan, 1926) 56.

[5]Funk, *Language*, p. 235.

Indeed, the Paul of the letters is an apocalyptic theologian, not a storyteller. Concepts and arguments must be understood before they can be appropriated. Language here functions in a different way from its use in the story or parable. A story, as told by Jesus, is to be understood in terms of its total impact. The response to a story is not: "What is the relation between the steps in the argument?" or "What do you mean?" Nor does our response consist of questions of cognitive, intellectual understanding. Rather our response to a story is immediate—a response of yes or no to its total impact.

For instance, when Jesus finishes his parable of the vineyard in Mark 12, the chief priests, scribes, and elders do not respond to it with an intellectual inquiry, but with an immediate emotional reaction: "When they realized that he had told this parable against them, they wanted to arrest him, but they feared the crowd. So they left him and went away" (Mark 12:12).

When surveying the ministry of Jesus, it becomes clear that he is not a theologian, but rather a man of religion. As a person who uses in his preaching the story, the proverb, and the parable, Jesus employs the stuff of this earth and of the common life. He interprets the realities of the created order in such a way that their sacral character is disclosed. What characterizes Jesus' religion is that he does not establish a rabbinical school in Nazareth; he does not point people to the Temple as the unique place of God's presence; he does not draw people into a monastery, like Qumran, to experience God. Rather, he discloses God's presence in every domain of the world of creation. In Jesus' perception of reality, our everyday, routinized world becomes a sacred reality; the secular becomes the sacred or, rather, the sacred permeates the secular and makes it the theater of God's active presence.

We know that the focus of Jesus' preaching was the dawning presence of the kingdom of God. But we must understand that Jesus' preaching of the coming kingdom is intimately related to the miracles he performs. Indeed, Jesus' word is enacted in his work. His healings are anticipatory manifestations of the coming kingdom of God, when the whole creation will be made whole. This becomes clear when Jesus integrates his exorcism—the casting out of demons representing the power of Satan in this world—with the actual presence of the kingdom of God: "If it is by the finger of God that I cast out the demons, then the kingdom of God has come to you" (Luke 11:20; cf. Matt. 12:38). And when the seventy disciples return to Jesus with the joyful report, "Lord, in your name even the demons submit to us," Jesus associates the submission of the demons with the fall of Satan, i.e., with the dawning presence of God's kingdom: "I watched Satan fall from heaven like a flash of lightning" (Luke 10:18).

Indeed, Jesus enacts the kingdom of God with its universal compassion in his ministry: *Already now*, the messianic banquet is celebrated in his dining with harlots and publicans; *already now*, God's forgiveness of the end time is manifested in Jesus' forgiveness of the common folk who transgress the stipulations of the Jewish law. In other words, it is in this world—in these concrete circumstances—that in Jesus' word and act God's presence is conveyed both in judgment and compassion.

However, we may wonder in what sense Jesus' preaching of the kingdom of God results in his suffering and death on the cross? Why wouldn't a preacher who announces the universal embrace of God's kingdom and who enacts God's immediate presence in his words and acts be the object of a wide popularity and amazement (cf. e.g., Mark 1:21; 2:12)? Why, then, did Jesus evoke from the very beginning of his ministry such a hostile reaction among the religious leaders of Israel (Mark 3:6)? This hostility is the reaction of an elitist, established religion that feels threatened by what it considers to be Jesus' subversive activity in overturning the hallowed tradition of Judaism. At least this is the way the gospel accounts portray the Judaism of the time. Bornkamm has stated—to be sure, with some exaggeration—that the newness of Jesus and his teachings consisted in the fact that he communicates God's immediate presence in judgment and mercy, whereas it was the tendency of Judaism to locate God either in the hallowed past (the Torah) or in the future (the messianic era to come).

It was indeed Jesus' claim to divine authority that provoked the hostility of the Jewish leaders. His authoritative claim interpreted the Torah in such a novel way that it broke the boundaries that Jewish tradition gave it. For how could Jesus claim authority to forgive sins? Notice how the scribes react to Jesus' forgiveness of a paralytic: "It is blasphemy! Who can forgive sins but God alone?" (Mark 2:7). Jesus' sovereign freedom in interpreting God's rule and will is nowhere more clearly described than in Mark 7, when Jesus responds to the complaint of the Pharisees that the disciples "do not live according to the tradition of the elders, but eat with defiled hands" (Mark 7:5) as follows: "Listen to me, all of you, and understand there is nothing outside a person that by going in can defile, but the things that come out are what defile. . . . Thus, he declared all foods clean" (Mark 7:14-15, 19).

And so the wide open extent of Jesus' proclamation of the will of God coupled with his authoritative claim to convey God's presence in the immediate present led to an increasingly hostile confrontation with the Jewish authorities, which finally led to his trial and death.

When we now raise the question of Jesus' significance for us, it strikes us in the first place that Jesus never argues for the existence of God nor for his transcendence, but instead conveys the already present God in our midst. Indeed, Jesus' language does not give so much new information about God, but rather creates a fresh awareness about God's presence. That awareness was so unlike the usual perceptions in which people were engaged that it gained ultimate significance—that of "God is here."

It is of crucial importance for us to recapture this perception of the historical Jesus; to regain a religious apperception of reality in a world where all of us are overwhelmed by a secular autonomy. Indeed, many of us have become theological giants but are ignorant about any religious quality in our lives. Jesus alerts us to those dimensions of life that we usually ignore—not only sensitivity and compassion to others, but also a new imagination in our dealing with God's creation so that we may gain a sense of wonder about its manifold beauty.

It seems to me especially harmful that our theological tradition has steered us away from this world, from responsibility for it and from protecting it against abuse. The dogmatic development of the Christian tradition no longer centered on Jesus' human life, but rather on issues of Jesus' preexistence and post-existence, which almost voided the human word and work of Jesus' ministry. Thus, the Apostolic Creed mentions only "Jesus' birth of the Holy Spirit and the Virgin Mary" and his crucifixion; the Nicene Creed (325 A.D.) has almost nothing to report about Jesus' life in the world: ". . . who was made flesh for our salvation and lived among men and suffered and rose again on the third day," whereas the Chalcedonian Creed (451 A.D.) so concentrates on the relation of the divine and the human nature of Christ that his historical life is not even mentioned.

The eclipse of Jesus' historical life in favor of Christological and Trinitarian definitions was accompanied by a dualistic worldview that turned all interest away from this world to the supranatural world. This Christian religiosity abandoned the world in the search for its heavenly home; it either demonized the world or viewed it as a necessary preamble to our real life in heaven. And so the world of God's creation was considered to be nothing but a fallen world, a vale of tears and folly. Persons were not truly human unless they were endowed with special supernatural gifts through the sacraments of the church. The dogmatic tradition, then, viewed the church as the place of grace in the midst of a fallen world, so that the church with its priestly apparatus became the only place where channels of grace were available in a corrupt, God-forsaken world. And so the Christian ideal became that of the monk who, in order to gain Christ, had to leave the world for the monastery.

Although the patristic tradition with its metaphysical tendencies is no longer prevalent among us, its influence is still present in many Christian circles. And we must not forget that it often betrayed the very things for which Jesus lived and died. First, it tended to dehumanize Jesus — to consider his life as a full human being to be unimportant as compared to his preexistent and post-existent status. Second, it tended to desacralize the world as God's creation. With the resurrection and ascension of Christ, "the spiritual" was, as it were, removed from the earth and located in a realm outside history that now became our true home and destiny. Thus, God's creation, where everything profoundly testifies to his care and presence in Jesus' view, now became a world of things to be conquered by the almighty human ego — it became an exclusively secular and technological world without any inherent worth. And third, it tended to disregard the sacred in the secular, and the concretization of human life that, as a psychosomatic reality, is profoundly intertwined with the stuff of the created world. The church tended to overspiritualize its life in dealing so much with heavenly realities that it had little concern for the dignity of the human being as the image of God in this world.

And so Christians should recapture what Jesus taught us and enacted for us: the presence of the sacred in the midst of ordinary life, perceived as the presence of the compassion and judgment of the God who sustains us amidst the world's joys and sufferings. But we should not entertain the illusion as if the way of Jesus is an easy way. That way will be as full of suffering in our time as it was in Jesus' time. For the world's craving for security and power will not allow the presence of any god but that of its own making. It will resist the surprising presence of the God of Jesus with its so different estimate of who deserves compassion and who deserves judgment.

It seems fitting to conclude with the profound words of Albert Schweitzer at the end of *The Quest of the Historical Jesus*, because they mirror what I have attempted to emphasize:

> He comes to us as the unknown, without a name, as of old, by the lake-side, He came to those men who knew Him not. He

speaks to us the same words: 'Follow thou me!' and sets us to the tasks which He has to fulfill for our time. He commands. And to those who obey Him, whether they be wise or simple, He will reveal Himself in the toils, the conflicts, the sufferings, which they shall pass through in His fellowship, and, as an ineffable mystery, they shall learn in their own experience who He is.[6]

---

[6]Schweitzer, *The Quest*, p. 403.

CHAPTER 9

The Gospel according to Mark

IT IS WIDELY RECOGNIZED TODAY THAT MARK IS THE EARLIEST written Gospel and was one of the sources for the other Synoptic Gospels, Matthew and Luke. However, before scholarship in the nineteenth century demonstrated the priority of Mark over Matthew and Luke, Mark was not given the place of honor among the Gospels in the history of the church.

According to Eusebius, in the beginning of the second century Papias posited Mark as the interpreter of Peter: "Mark was an interpreter [*hermeneutes*] of Peter and wrote down carefully what he remembered—though not in order—what was said or done by the Lord" (*H.E.* iii, 39, 15). However, scholarship has disputed the reliability of this report: "As justification for the tradition attested by Papias that John Mark is the author of Mark, one can adduce the fact that obviously the tendency to attribute the Gospels to personal followers of Jesus arose quite early."[1]

Moreover, Augustine's judgment that the Gospels originated in the same order as they are found in the canon and that the later Gospels were not written without knowledge of the earlier ones, which made him conclude that Mark was an abbreviation of Matthew, was subsequently widely accepted in the history of the church.

Even more surprising is the fact that—given the intense preoccupation of scholarship with Mark in recent times—no explicit citation from Mark occurs in the post-apostolic church before Justin Martyr (156 A.D.) and Irenaeus (180 A.D.). The popularity of both Matthew and Luke clearly overshadowed Mark in the patristic period.

---

[1]W. G. Kümmel, *Introduction*, p. 97.

Outline of the Gospel[2]

A. The Mystery of the Kingdom, 1:1—4:34
B. The Blindness of the Disciples, 4:35—8:21
C. The Suffering of the Son of Man, 8:22—10:52
D. The End of the Temple, 11:1—13:37
E. The Passion and Resurrection of Jesus, 14:1—16:8

Distinctive Marks of the Gospel

THE TITLE OF THE GOSPEL "THE BEGINNING OF THE GOSPEL of Jesus Christ, the Son of God" (1:1) is remarkable in several respects. Mark seems to have been the first Christian to create the novel literary product of a written gospel. Prior to Mark's creation of the gospel as a written narrative of the deeds and words of Jesus, the term gospel had been exclusively reserved for the oral proclamation of the gospel. This is especially clear in Paul's use of the term. In 1 Cor. 15:1-5, Paul not only speaks about his oral preaching of the gospel (verse 1), but also tells the Corinthians that the oral transmission of the gospel was a common tradition in the church: "For I handed on to you as of first importance what I in turned had received" (verse 3). The novelty of Mark's literary achievement is that he not only shifts the traditional meaning of the core of the gospel, that is, the proclamation of the death and resurrection of Christ from oral proclamation to a written narrative, but also creates a continuous narrative of the life of Jesus from the beginning of his ministry to its end in his death and resurrection.

The frequency with which Mark uses the noun "gospel" (*euangelion*; 1:1, 14-15; 8:35; 10:29; 13:10; 14:9) is remarkable, especially when we compare his use with that of the other Synoptic Gospels and John. In both Luke and John the term is absent, whereas Matthew gives it a specific content—"the gospel of the kingdom" (4:33; 9:35; cf. "this gospel" in 24:14 and 28:13). In fact, Luke calls his gospel-narrative not a "gospel," but a "narrative" (*diēgēsis*; 1:1).

Although it is clear that Mark is familiar with the traditional meaning of "the gospel" as oral proclamation (1:14; 13:10; 14:9), his use of the term for the kerygmatic presentation of the life of Jesus constitutes his

---

[2]My outline follows that of Werner H. Kelber, except for the last section (14:1—16:8; *Mark's Story of Jesus* (Philadelphia: Fortress Press, 1979) 7–8.

novel creation. This novel comprehensive use of the term is apparent in 1:1, 15; 8:35, and 10:29. In fact, in both 8:35 and 10:29, Mark identifies the life and death of Jesus explicitly with the term gospel, when Jesus defines discipleship in terms of "for my sake and the gospel."

But why, the reader may ask, does Mark specify the title of his Gospel as "the *beginning* of the gospel of Jesus Christ, the Son of God"? In what sense can the narrative of Jesus be the beginning of the gospel? Several solutions to this problematic element in the title have been suggested. Kelber, for example, writes:

> He [Mark] regards the total written story as the beginning of the gospel. The Markan text prepares the reader for the appropriation of the gospel message. It is only after the gospel story has been read from start to finish that the reader knows Mark's gospel message and can adopt it for his or her life situation. In this sense, reading the Gospel of Mark is but the beginning of the gospel's actualization in real life.[3]

Notwithstanding this intriguing hermeneutical move that Kelber attributes to Mark, it seems more adequate to refer the problematic term "the beginning" to Mark's introduction of Jesus' ministry, which does not commence until we reach 1:15. In other words, the beginning of the gospel is constituted not only by the Old Testament promise (verses 2 and 3), but also by Jesus' forerunner—by the preaching of John the Baptist and his baptism of Jesus (verses 4–11).

What are the characteristic marks of Mark's Gospel? We must recognize that Mark is not only a collector of prior oral Christian traditions—which may even include some written traditions—but also a creative theologian.

It is impossible to determine Mark's theological achievement unless we recognize his function as a collector. Indeed, his Gospel is marked by his collection of a variety of oral traditions which he subsequently rearranged according to his own narrative purpose.

> Mark inherited a cycle of miracle stories portraying Jesus as exhibiting the traits of a Hellenistic "divine man," the stories now in Mark 5 and 7. Further, a cycle of controversy stories in Mark 2 concerning forgiveness of sins, eating with tax collectors and

---

[3]Ibid., p. 16.

sinners, fasting and keeping the Sabbath lack evidence of specifically Markan literary traits in the way they are linked together, and Mark may well have inherited them as a unit. It is also probable that Mark inherited the collection of parables now in Mark 4 as a collection.[4]

However, Mark is not simply a collector of traditions about Jesus; he not only devised a way of connecting these traditions into a narrative whole, but also stamped them with his own theological perspective. For instance, Mark provides the traditional units with his own summaries, which occur as transitions in the narrative (1:14-15, 21-22, 39; 2:13; 3:7-12; 5:21; 6:6b, 12-13, 30-33, 53-56; 10:1). Moreover, he constructs interesting geographical references to mark the movement of his narrative: "From 1:14 to 6:13 we are in Galilee; from 6:14 to 8:26 beyond Galilee; from 8:27 to 10:52 moving from Caesarea Philippi to Jerusalem and from 11:1 to 16:8 we are in Jerusalem."[5]

What is especially noteworthy is Mark's use of sophisticated symbolisms. References to the numbers 3, 7, and 12 carry a special salvation-historical value. For instance, the number 3 occurs in 8:31; 9:31; 10:34 (the number 6 [2 x 3] in 9:2), the number 7 in 8:5-8, and the number 12 in 6:43. And the scenes at the lakeside and Jesus' repeated travels by boat refer symbolically to the forthcoming spread of the gospel beyond the boundaries of Israel to the Gentile world.

Mark's theological creativity can be summarized by pointing to three themes that pervade his Gospel:
(1) the theology of suffering
(2) the mystery of Jesus' identity
(3) the theme of discipleship
After discussing the first theme separately, I will treat the other two themes together, although we must remember that all three themes are closely interwoven.

Mark's narrative is dominated by the motif of "the way," tracing Jesus' journey from Galilee to Jerusalem, the place of his final destiny. "The way" motif opens the story of the gospel by citing the Old Testament prophets in 1:2-3 : "See, I am sending my messenger ahead of you,

[4]Norman Perrin, *The New Testament: An Introduction* (New York: Harcourt Brace Jovanovich, 1974) 234.
[5]Ibid., p. 239.

who will prepare your way. . . . Prepare the way of the Lord" (Mal. 3:1; Isa. 40:3) and receives heightened emphasis in sections 3 and 4 of the Gospel (8:22—10:52; 11:1—13:37) when Jesus is "on the way" to his passion in Jerusalem. So Jesus asks his disciples "on the way" (8:27a): "Who do people say that I am?" (8:27b) which evokes Peter's confession "You are the Messiah" (8:29). Again, in the context of Jesus' prediction of his passion (9:30-32), he asks the disciples, "What were you arguing about 'on the way?'" (9:33). However, in both cases, the disciples misunderstand the way of Jesus: Peter does not want to acknowledge the forthcoming death of Jesus (8:31-33), whereas the disciples spend their time— while they are "on the way"—in discussing "who was the greatest" among them (9:34). And Jesus' firm resolve to travel the way to Jerusalem is met by "fear and amazement" on the part of the disciples (10:32).

Indeed, the basic storyline in Mark is Jesus' impending passion and death. It has been said that the Gospel of Mark is "a passion narrative with an extended introduction,"[6] and that Mark composed his Gospel "backward" from the passion narrative.[7] Although these statements undermine the import of the first half of Mark's Gospel with its emphasis on Jesus' unique authority and with its many miracle stories which the evangelist purposely has included in his narrative, they represent nevertheless a correct estimate of Mark's basic strategy. As Perrin observes: "Every major section of the Gospel ends on a note looking toward the passion, and the control section, 8:27—10:45, is concerned with interpreting it:

3:6: The plot 'to destroy Jesus';
6:6: The unbelief of the people of 'his own country';
8:21: The misunderstanding of the disciples;
10:45: The cross as 'a ransom for many';
12:44: The widow's sacrifice, which anticipates Jesus'."[8]

Mark has often been characterized as "the Pauline gospel," because of his so-called dominant emphasis on the cross of Christ. Yet Mark resembles more the theology of 1 Peter (see later) than that of Paul. Both Mark and 1 Peter are theologians of the sufferings of Christ rather than theologians of the cross, although the words of the angel, "You are look-

---

[6]Martin Kähler, *The So-called Historical Jesus and the Historic, Biblical Christ*, trans. C. Braaten (Philadelphia: Fortress Press, 1964) 80, n.11.
[7]Willi Marxsen, *Mark the Evangelist*, trans. J. Boyce, et al. (Nashville: Abingdon Press, 1969) 31.
[8]Perrin, *The New Testament*, p. 240.

ing for Jesus of Nazareth, who was crucified. He has been raised; he is not here" (16:6)—have a Pauline connotation. Mark's intent becomes clear in a saying like, "If any want to become my followers, let them deny themselves and take up their cross and follow me" (8:34; cf. Matt. 10:38; 16:24; Luke 9:23 "daily"; 14:27).

The passion of Christ becomes in Mark the paradigm for Christian discipleship: All the passion predictions in Mark (8:38; 9:31; 10:30) point to "following Jesus on the way [to the cross]" (cf. also 10:21, 52). Indeed, the close relationship between the suffering of Christ and discipleship is so strongly emphasized in Mark, because the community he addresses is involved in suffering and needs to understand that the way of discipleship is the way of Christ: from suffering to glory.

The issue of Jesus' identity is inseparably connected with the issue of discipleship, and both issues culminate in Mark's theology of suffering (see above).

The problem of Jesus' identity in Mark was decisively clarified in 1901 by W. Wrede's *Das Messiasgeheimnis in den Evangelien*.[9] Wrede contends that the messianic secret in Mark is not anchored in the life of the historical Jesus, but is rather a dogmatic construct of the evangelist. It contains three elements: (1) The command of Jesus to silence demons (1:25, 34; 3:12), and to order people whom he healed (1:43-45; 5:43; 7:36; 8:26) and the disciples (8:30; 9:9) not to reveal his messianic dignity. (2) The repeated remarks about the misunderstanding and lack of faith of the disciples (cf., e.g., 4:13, 40-41). (3) Mark's theory of the parables (4:10-13), which emphasizes that the mystery of the kingdom is reserved for insiders.

Indeed, "in Mark's Gospel, Jesus' identity is not immediately apparent to the human characters in the story. Only the demons know that Jesus is the Son of God since they are supernatural beings, but Jesus silences them."[10] Mark employs the device of the messianic secret to emphasize that God's revelation in Jesus Christ can only be fully understood after the passion and resurrection of Christ. Thus, the messianic secret operates as an obstacle, so as not to view Jesus' miracles in terms of an obvious epiphany of his status as Son of God apart from his passion and the disciple's way of suffering. Within the context of the mystery of

---

[9]Translated into English under the title, *The Messianic Secret* (London: James Clark, 1971).

[10]Frank J. Matera, *What Are They Saying about Mark?* (New York: Paulist Press, 1987) 22.

Jesus' identity the irony of Mark's narrative surfaces. It is apparent not only in the misunderstanding of the crowds who "follow" Jesus because of his miraculous glorious deeds (2:15; 3:7), but especially in the continuous misunderstanding of the twelve disciples, who are appointed by Jesus to assist him in his mission (3:13-19), but who desire the way of glory and not the way of suffering. Mark strongly accentuates this misunderstanding of the disciples (4:13b, 40; 6:52; 8:14-21; 9:6, 10, 32; 10:32; 14:40b) which finally leads to their apostasy and fatal betrayal of Jesus. Even Peter's confession of Jesus as Messiah manifests his blindness—a blindness that becomes even worse in the sequence of the narrative.

After his glorification on the mountain (9:2-8), Jesus "ordered them [Peter, James, and John] to tell no one about what they had seen, until the Son of Man had risen from the dead. So they kept the matter to themselves, questioning what this rising from the dead could mean" (9:9-10). In what follows this scene, the misunderstanding of the three disciples becomes apparent: They fail to grasp that Jesus' glorification can only take place after his passion (9:10-13). And so Kelber may be correct when he writes: "[Jesus'] disciples not unexpectedly 'all forsook him and fled' (14:50), the very moment the opponents lay hands on him. They had *all* drunk of the cup (14:23), they had *all* pledged to die with him (14:31), yet they *all* abandon him at the outset of his passion (14:50). Not following Jesus, they cannot reach the goal of the way. Their flight marks the end of their way of discipleship."[11]

The irony in Mark's Gospel becomes clear when we realize that insiders become outsiders, whereas outsiders become insiders. Thus while the Jewish authorities—Jesus' co-religionists—and Jesus' own disciples either plan to destroy him or to betray him, there are two conspicuous "outsiders," who "see" the nature of Jesus' true identity. The first outsider is the blind Bartimaeus, who appears in the Gospel immediately prior to the beginning of the passion story in chapter 11 when Jesus arrives in Jerusalem (10:46-52).

This blind man represents symbolically the true believer—the insider who has "insight" into what it means to follow Jesus on his way to the passion: "Immediately he regained his sight and followed him on the way" (10:52). Just as the blind Bartimaeus becomes a symbol of the true follower of Jesus at the beginning of Jesus' way to the cross, so the

---

[11]Kelber, *Mark's Story of Jesus*, p. 77.

Roman centurion becomes the true confessor of Jesus' real identity at the end of the passion story: "Truly this man was God's Son" (15:39).

It is a remarkable touch of Mark's irony that both an arbitary blind man sitting "by the roadside" (10:46) and a gentile centurion become true believers and insiders, whereas those who were supposed to be privileged "insiders" are put to shame and remain blind to Jesus' real identity.

CHAPTER 10

The Gospel according
to Matthew

SINCE ITS RECEPTION IN THE CANON, MATTHEW HAS BEEN THE most influential of all the Gospels in the history of the church. In fact, since the era of the Apostolic Fathers, it has been the most cited Gospel in the early church. The first commentary on the Sermon on the Mount was produced by Augustine, who was probably the first person to refer to Matthew 5–7 as "the Sermon on the Mount." Later Thomas Aquinas, Luther, and Calvin followed him in this manner. Until the nineteenth century, with the advent of the two-source theory of the Synoptic Gospels, Matthew was considered to be not only *the primary* Gospel in terms of influence and importance, but also *the original* Gospel, that is, the first written Gospel — copied by Luke and abbreviated by Mark.[1]

Didactic Emphasis

THE INFLUENCE OF MATTHEW IS EASILY UNDERSTANDABLE. MOST Christians mean "Matthew" when they refer to the teachings of Jesus. Where else do we find such an elaborate and orderly account of Jesus' teaching — such didactic emphasis? Where else such sustained blocks of teaching, such a coherent literary composition? Notice, for instance, the five blocks of teaching — ordered almost like the Pentateuch of Moses, a new Torah by Jesus, the New Moses, giving his law on a new Sinai, the Sermon on the Mount. These five blocks comprise chapters 5–7 (the

---

[1]Cf. Augustine and many other Roman Catholic scholars: "Mark the abbreviator of Matthew."

Sermon on the Mount); chapter 10 (the mission–discourse); chapter 13 (the parable chapter); chapter 18 (on church order); and 24:1 – 25:46 (the eschatological discourse). Each block ends with the stereotyped phrase: "Now when Jesus had finished sayings these things. . . ."[2]

However, another way to construe Matthew's Gospel is to structure it around the identical phrases of 4:17 and 16:21: "From that time Jesus began to proclaim, 'Repent, for the kingdom of heaven has come near'" (4:17); "From that time on, Jesus began to show his disciples that he must go to Jerusalem and undergo great suffering" (16:21). Therefore, I suggest the following structure of the Gospel:

A. The Origin of Jesus–Messiah, 1:1 – 4:16

B. Jesus' Galilean ministry, 4:17 – 10:42 ordered around *teaching* (chapters 5–7) and *healing* (chapters 8–9); Jesus' charge to ministry as model for the apostles' mission (chapter 10)

C. Rejection by Jewish opponents and the glimmering faith of the disciples, 11:1 – 16:20 (cf. 16:13-20; Peter's confession at Caesarea Philippi)

D. On the Way to Jerusalem, 16:21 – 20:34

E. Passion and Resurrection, 21:1 – 28:15

F. Charge to the Disciples, 28:16-20

The length and order of teaching in Matthew are especially conspicuous when we compare it with the brevity of teaching material in Mark and the much more diffuse character and organization of Luke's Gospel (cf. especially Matthew's and Luke's differing ordering of Q [their common Sayings-Source]).

Matthew is indeed a didactic Gospel. Because of its usefulness for catechetical instruction, it was used prominently in the early church (cf., e.g., the *Didache* [an early church manual ca. 100] and its catechism of the Two Ways; cf. also the *Epistles of Barnabas* and *1 Clement*).

It is not only the difference in length that strikes us, or the fullness of teaching material in Matthew compared to Mark, but especially its different overall focus. Mark focuses on a paradoxical epistemology, that is, on the issue of the blindness of the old age and on the new perception of

---

[2]7:28, 11:1; 13:53; 19:1; 26:1. B. W. Bacon devised the structure of Matthew as a new Pentateuch. Although attractive, it is both too rigid and deficient: it does not give room to chapter 23, and it reduces the infancy-narratives and the passion-narrative as prologue and epilogue, minimizing their crucial importance for Matthew.

God's glory in the death of Christ (cf. especially the crucial mid-section of Mark's Gospel [8:22—10:52], which is preoccupied with the themes of sight and blindness). Thus while Mark's preoccupation with epistemology is close to the concern of the Gospel of John, Matthew's focus lies elsewhere. What concerns him is the question of the will and action of believers, that is, the issue of obedience and praxis. In short, Matthew focuses on the question whether we will or will not follow Jesus' teaching and—in so following it—follow him on the way to the cross. In other words, whereas Mark and John focus on the question, Do you *see* the light which shines in our darkness? Matthew's concern is, Will you *execute* the greater righteousness and "perfection," which Jesus-Messiah-Son of God requires (5:20, 48)?

We must be aware then that the term *righteousness* has in Matthew a very different connotation from that in Paul. In Matthew righteousness is a matter of *becoming* and *doing* and only then one of *being*, that is, of "being righteous."[3] In Paul, righteousness is first of all a question of *being*, or rather of the reception of (grace and) righteousness, which subsequently must issue in *doing* "works" of righteousness, or exhibiting "the fruit" of righteousness.

The Church

IN ADDITION TO MATTHEW'S DIDACTIC FOCUS, NO OTHER GOSPEL deals so explicitly with the *church* and with its polity (cf. 18:15-20). The specific identity and the authenticity of the church is a main concern in Matthew. It is the church of Jesus Christ, the lowly Messiah on earth and the exalted Messiah in heaven after his resurrection, the one "who is gentle and humble in heart" and whose "yoke is easy and whose burden is light" (11:29-30), the one who fulfills Zechariah 9:9 by entering Jerusalem "humble, and mounted on a donkey" (21:5), but the one who is *also* the mighty "*Lord*" both in the *miracle stories* (chapters 8–9; 14:30) and in his authoritative teaching (7:20-29).

Thus Matthew is not only a *didactic* Gospel, but an *ecclesial* Gospel as well. Indeed, he alone of the Synoptic Gospels and John mentions the concept "church" (*ekklēsia*) and does so in two crucial texts: in the context of Peter's confession and Jesus' promise that "on this rock I will build my church, and the gates of Hades will not prevail against it" (16:18),

---

[3]*Dikaiosynē* occurs seven times in Matthew: 3:15; 5:6, 10, 20; 6:1, 33; 21:32.

and again in Jesus' discussion of the internal order of the church, where the church becomes the final arbiter in excommunicating unrepentant believers, since it has the apostolic power to "bind and loose" on earth what will be bound in heaven (18:18). In this context belong also texts like 18:20 and 28:20. In 18:20 Jesus promises "where two or three are gathered in my name, I am there among them," and in 28:20 Jesus assures the church "I am with you always, to the end of the age."

The identity of the church is defined over against a double threat which imperils its existence—a threat from the outside and one from within. The threat from the outside is caused by the synagogue. In Matthew it is always referred to as *"their/your* synagogue," as if Jesus himself and his disciples are engaged with an alien body of Jews, to which they — even as Jews—do not belong.[4]

The threat from within is that of spiritual disorder and is directed against false teachers of the law who relax the requirement of the Law (chapter 23), and against false prophets (7:15-23; 24:24-26) who, notwithstanding their miraculous activity, are characterized as "ravenous wolves" (7:15). Moreover, Matthew frequently calls the Jewish leaders (the Pharisees) "hypocrites."[5]

At this point we must raise a serious question about Matthew's church. What actually constitutes its unique and authentic character? Has it separated itself completely from its mother church, Pharisaic Judaism, or does it still live within the framework of Judaism as a separate sect as-it-were and thus in a broken relation to its parent? This question arises because the church still practices Jewish tithing (23:23), keeps the Sabbath (24:20), and pays the temple tax (17:24-27). It seems as if the church is only a more consistent form of Judaism. It is admonished to obey Pharisaic theology (23:2) and must *practice* what the Pharisees, who sit on Moses' seat, only *preach* (23:1). Indeed, how different is the identity of the church in John! In contrast to Matthew's bitter and sometimes ambivalent dialogue with Judaism, in John open hostility and a total break with the parent religion prevails. John actually characterizes Judaism as satanic (chapter 8). And so John represents a stage which surpasses that of Matthew in terms of the relation between Judaism and Christianity because

---

[4]Cf. 4:23; 9:35; 10:17; 12:9; 13:54; cf. 23:34. The phrase occurs only twice in Mark (1:23, 39) and only once in Luke (4:15).
[5]This occurs fourteen times: 6:25; 7:5; 15:17; 22:18; 23:13, 15, 23, 25, 27, 28-29; 24:15.

John manifests the total separation between the two confessions after the Council of Jamnia (90 A.D.).

However, it is curious that neither Matthew nor John is interested in an explicit church order or in institutional safeguards.[6] The terminology of "apostle" does not appear in Matthew (except in 10:2), whereas we hear only incidentally about the presence of "prophets, sages, and scribes" (23:34). Although Peter is the rock of the church in Matthew and carries the authority of "binding and loosing" (16:18-20), he functions throughout the Gospel simply as the spokesman for all disciples (15:15; 16:35; 18:21; 19:27). And even Peter "the rock" is royally rebuked for his misunderstanding of Jesus' messianic role (16:22-23) and for his betrayal of him (26:69-75).

Discipleship

Introduction. Matthew's conception of the church as an egalitarian fellowship is reinforced by his strong emphasis on discipleship. We must notice that for Matthew, in contrast to the other New Testament books, the Christian believer is and remains a disciple (*mathētēs*).

Indeed, the mark of the Christian is discipleship, even after Jesus' resurrection. And so we can say that in Matthew, the *ear-witness* of the *disciples*—their hearing and obeying—displaces as-it-were the *eyewitness* of the *apostles* in Luke-Acts—that is, their witness to the resurrection of Jesus (Luke 24:48; Acts 1:8, 22; 13:31).[7] Discipleship is not only applicable to the contemporary companions of Jesus' ministry, but to all believers in general (28:20). Thus discipleship transcends historical distance. Kierkegaard's question about whether "the contemporary disciple" has an advantage over "the disciple at second hand" is answered in Matthew in a much simpler way than by Kierkegaard.[8] For Matthew every Christian must always become contemporaneous with the Jesus who has become the Christ. Indeed, a Christian is here defined as one who *hears* and *does* what Jesus has commanded: "teaching them [the nations] to obey everything that I have commanded you" (28:20).

---

[6]In John the church is constituted by a group of "spiritual" people (*pneumatikoi*), symbolized by the Beloved Disciple.
[7]Cf. also Paul: 1 Cor. 9:1, "Have I not seen Jesus our Lord?" 1 Cor. 15:5-9.
[8]S. Kierkegaard, *Philosophical Fragments* (Princeton, N.J.: Princeton University Press, 1962) chaps. 4–5.

Thus true hearing is measured by the praxis of the disciple: "A disciple is not above the teacher, nor a slave above the master; it is enough for the disciple to be like the teacher" (10:24-25), and "You are not to be called rabbi, for you have one teacher, and you are all students" (23:8). And so the task of the disciples after Jesus' resurrection and exaltation becomes "discipleing," that is, "to make *disciples* (*mathēteusate*) of all nations" (28:19).

Permanent Discipleship. Matthew's emphasis on "permanent" discipleship is impressive. He uses the word "disciple" sixty-five times; moreover, he has it forty-five times without parallels in Mark and Luke. In contrast to Luke, Matthew limits the circle of disciples to the Twelve.[9] Whereas Luke reports: "He called his disciples and chose from twelve of them, whom he also named apostles" (6:13), Matthew states in the parallel text simply: "Then he summoned his twelve disciples" (10:1). The disciples are contrasted to "the people" and "the crowds" (but see 5:1) since it is only they who are given to understand Jesus: "To you it has been given to know the secrets of the kingdom of heaven, but to them it has not been given." (13:11). Thus the disciples call Jesus "Lord," whereas the crowds call Jesus "teacher."

The Distinctiveness of Discipleship. The distinctive features of Matthew's description of discipleship are as follows: first the democratization of the church. In contrast to the hierarchical structure of the synagogue, the church is simply a company of disciples (see above).

Next, the ideal disciple is the Christian scribe who "brings out of his treasure what is new and what is old" (13:52). Indeed, this democratic fellowship is built on the principle of *continuity* in the midst of *discontinuity*: the new is not so much the abrogation of the old order (cf. Rom. 10:4), but rather its fulfillment and climax (Matt. 5:17-20). Just as Scripture legitimates Jesus as the Messiah, so the true intent of the Old Testament Law legitimates Jesus' teaching of the kingdom in opposition to the Pharisees (cf. especially Matthew's frequent fulfillment-citations: 1:22; 2:6; 4:14; 8:17; 12:17; 13:35; 21:4; 26:54-56; 27:9).

The third feature is the radical pragmatism of discipleship. It is not spiritualized or defined as "being in Christ" (cf. Paul), but rather con-

---

[9]See Luke 6:17, "a great crowd of his disciples" and Luke 19:37, "the whole multitude of disciples."

cretized as *imitatio Christi*. Hence the verb "to follow" is so central in the Gospel (20 times). It refers to following in Jesus' footsteps, a following that is profoundly illustrated in Jesus' charge to the young rich man: "If you wish to be perfect, go, sell your possessions, and give the money to the poor, and you will have treasure in heaven; then come, follow me" (19:21). The radicality of this discipleship is furthermore demonstrated by the sequel to the story of the rich young man (19:16-22). Peter confesses: "Look, we have left everything and followed you" (19:27), whereupon Jesus promises eternal life to those "who have followed me," that is, to "everyone who has left houses or brothers or sisters or father or mother or children or fields, for my name's sake" (19:29). And so discipleship becomes a life of leaving all worldly securities behind and of becoming wanderers on earth for the sake of the kingdom of God.

Fourth, the radical pragmatism of discipleship is connected with an interesting christological criterion. It is instructive to compare Matthew with John, Paul, and Mark in this respect. In John true faith is the acknowledgment of "seeing" Jesus as the Son of God incarnate—seeing the "glory of God" in Jesus' human form, and in seeing through his empirical miracles Jesus as the unique and only begotten Son of the Father. In Paul, however, saving faith is faith in the death and resurrection of Christ as the sole ground of salvation in opposition to the works of the Law, while in Mark saving faith is primarily a new epistemological perception.

However, in Matthew saving faith depends on the inseparable bond between faith and action; not by faith alone or by action alone, but by the action without which faith is empty. Thus Matthew has Jesus say: "Not everyone who says to me, 'Lord, Lord,' will enter the kingdom of heaven, but only the one who *does* the will of my Father in heaven" (7:21). Matthew and the Epistle of James agree on this matter, notwithstanding their so different historical locations. Indeed, Matthew seems to elaborate on a statement by James: "But if any are hearers of the word and not doers, they are like those who look at themselves in a mirror. . . . But those who look into the perfect law, the law of liberty, and persevere, being not hearers who forget, but *doers who act*, they will be blessed in their *doing*" (James 1:23, 25).

And so Matthew's christological criterion can be characterized simply as this: Are you a good apple or a rotten apple in your daily life? In other words, the only valid criterion is that of good fruit: "You will know them by their fruits. Are grapes gathered from thorns, or figs from thistles?" (7:16-17); "Either make the tree good, and its fruit good; or make the tree bad, and its fruit bad, for the tree is known by its fruit"

(12:33). Indeed, the mystery of Matthew's Christianity is how to be a good apple. For to be a good apple implies being rooted in a good tree. It is decided by the question whether you have solid roots, that is, whether your roots are anchored in Jesus the Messiah and in his proclamation of the kingdom of heaven.

In other words, do you believe Jesus' interpretation of God's will and his authority to bring about the dawning presence of God's kingdom? But just as faith and trust in Jesus' word and action determines one's entrance into the Kingdom—a faith such as that exhibited by the Gentile centurion (8:5f) and the Canaanite woman (15:21)—faith remains empty without "leaving everything behind," that is, without committing one's lifestyle completely to the way of Jesus. Thus discipleship in Matthew emphasizes, in Bonhoeffer's phrase, "the cost of discipleship." It means investing spiritual wealth into material poverty. Disciples are truly beggars in the world without "gold, or silver, or copper in your belts" (10:9). However, discipleship also means "perfection" (5:48; 19:21), the perfection of "doing" (7:12, 17-19, 21, 24, 26). Accordingly, Matthew does not indict pharisaic hypocrisy primarily because of its interpretation of the law, that is, because of its hermeneutical skill, but because of its contradiction between preaching and practice (23:3).

However, the split between pharisaic preaching and practice distorts as well its interpretation of the law. Thus Jesus charges the Pharisees with neglecting "the weightier matters of the law: justice and mercy and faith. It is these you ought to have practiced without neglecting the others" (23:23). And so the Pharisees violate the prophetic insight of Hosea 6:6: "I desire mercy, not sacrifice" (9:13; 12:7).

Notwithstanding Matthew's emphasis on perfection, the Christian is not characterized as the perfected disciple. Instead Matthew underscores the need for persistence and perseverance in discipleship. What counts is *becoming* perfect during one's pilgrimage in the world so that one is approved at last by the Son of God at the time of the Last Judgment.

Since the church is a mixture of good and evil (13:47-50), membership in it is no safeguard for salvation. This Matthew declares after narrating the parable of the invited guest who comes to the marriage-feast without proper attire and is therefore "thrown into the outer darkness. . . . For many are called, but few are chosen" (22:14; cf. also 8:11-12; 19:30; 20:16). The same message is sounded in the parables of the fishnet and the weeds (chapter 13). Moreover, Matthew expands the apocalyptic discourse of Mark 13 by adding three parables that carry the same message; the parables of the ten maidens (25:1-13), of the talents (25:14-30), and of the sheep and the goats (25:31-46). They all emphasize that although the coming of the Kingdom may be delayed, eternal bliss and condemnation will depend on one's perseverance and moral action. In other words, the delay of the coming of the Kingdom and the need for perseverance constitute a dialectic of patience and impatience: "This generation will not pass away until all these things (the coming of the Son of Man) have taken place" (24:34) and thus "the one who endures to the end will be saved" (24:13).

And finally—in conjunction with the theme of endurance and persistence—Matthew develops as well a *psychology of discipleship* which is unique in the New Testament. It comes to expression in two episodes at sea: "the stilling of the storm" (8:22-27) and "Jesus walking on the water" (14:22-33). Although both stories report a miraculous event, their focus is not the miracle, but the nature of discipleship. In the middle of the miracle chapter—chapter 8, containing ten healings—the issue of following Jesus suddenly arises and is answered in a radical way: "Follow me, and let the dead bury their own dead" (8:22). Immediately following is a boat scene. A great storm occurs, the boat is swamped by the waves while Jesus is asleep. The disciples shout in fear: "Lord save us! We are perishing!" They awaken Jesus who responds—*before* he stills the storm (in contrast to Mark 4:39)—with the words: "Why are you afraid, you of little faith?" (8:26).

There is another boat scene in 14:22-33. The boat is beaten by the waves, Jesus comes to the disciples, walking on the sea. The disciples utter a cry of fear; Peter obeys Jesus' command to come to him, walking on the water. He starts out in full faith, but then the text reports: "When he noticed the strong wind, he became frightened, and beginning to sink, he cried out, 'Lord, save me' " (verse 30). However, Jesus reaches out his hand, catches him, and says: "You of little faith, why did you doubt?" (verse 31).

For Matthew, the boat represents the church, which suffers great distress in a world that is hostile to the gospel, and the disciples in the boat are people in fear who must depend on Jesus' presence alone in the midst of the world's stormy waves (18:20; 28:20); cf. Calvin's characterization of the church: *Tranquillus saevis in undis* ["Tranquil amidst the stormy waves"]).

Matthew's psychology of discipleship comes also to expression when he emphasizes that there are *various degrees* of faith. He lives in a time when questions of doubt are being raised about the end time coming of Jesus (the Parousia; 24:48; 25:5). In fact, Matthew alone among the

New Testament writers mentions the doubt of believers, even at the time of Jesus' resurrection (28:17; cf. 14:31, above). Indeed doubt is a mark of "little faith"—a term that only Matthew uses (see 6:30; 8:26; 14:31; 16:8; 17:20). However, "little faith" is not the basic sin of apostasy and hypocrisy exhibited by the Pharisees and the false prophets (7:15; 23:2; 24:24), but is rather "halfway" faith. Matthew addresses this "halfway" faith by calling for endurance and watchfulness (24:12-13, 42-43; 25:13; 26:38, 40-41). Indeed, true faith overcomes doubt and fear (6:25), because it is forever vigilant: "stay awake and pray" (26:41).

Conclusion

IN CONTRAST TO THE CATHEDRAL SCENES OF JOHN (SEE LATER) and Ephesians with their liturgical celebrations and priestly solemnity, Matthew's Gospel transplants us to the Christian *Beth ha-Midrash*—the catechetical school of learning.

Its didactic character conveys to us the meaning and mandate of Christian discipleship. The difficulty Matthew causes us is not its intellectual depth or its mysterious character, but rather its inescapable simplicity. Indeed, the gospel's profundity is not located in its complexity, but rather in its simplicity. For its radical simplicity makes it offensive and difficult for us—an offense and difficulty not for our intellect, but for our lifestyle and action.

So Matthew reminds us of the mystery of the gospel in his own way, showing that the sole mark of our integrity as Christians is constituted by the conformity between word and deed in our lives. This integrity coupled with Matthew's ethical stringency was well understod by Christians such as Francis of Assisi, Leo Tolstoy, and Dietrich Bonhoeffer!

CHAPTER 11

The Gospel according to Luke and the Book of Acts

Preface

SINCE THE TWO-VOLUME WORK OF LUKE-ACTS COVERS FIFTY-TWO chapters and occupies one-fourth of the New Testament, it is not an easy task to give these books their proper due. In this chapter my main concern will be with the Book of Acts, especially with its portrait of Paul. Indeed, any study of the third Gospel must ultimately lead to its sequel, "for the evangelist certainly intended these books to be read together."[1]

Luke 1:1-4 serves as an introduction to both books and is taken up again in Acts 1:1-2: "In the first book, Theophilus (cf. Luke 1:3), I wrote about all that Jesus did and taught from the beginning until the day when he was taken up to heaven." The preface of the Gospel (Luke 1:1-4) indicates that Luke intends to supplant other gospel accounts and to write a normative, canonical gospel: "Since many have undertaken to set down an orderly account of the events that have been fulfilled among us, . . . I too decided, after investigating everything carefully from the very first, to write an orderly account for you, most excellent Theophilus, so that you may know the truth concerning the things about which you have been instructed."[2]

As Fitzmyer remarks: "The prologue has to be understood in relation

---

[1]Mark A. Powell, *What Are They Saying about Luke?* (New York: Paulist Press, 1989) 121.
[2]*The Gospel according to Luke (I-IX)* translated by Joseph A. Fitzmyer (AB; Garden City, N.Y.: Doubleday, 1981) 287.

to that of Acts, which explicitly names Jesus, unlike the prologue of the first volume. Furthermore, it has to be related to the two volumes as a whole, for the 'events' (1:1) in the two of them are subject matter of his 'narrative' (1:3)."[3]

Outline of Luke-Acts

I. The Gospel
   A. Prologue, 1:1-4
   B. Introducing Jesus' Ministry, 1:5—4:13
      1. The Infancy Narrative, 1:5—2:52
      2. Preparation for Jesus' Ministry, 3:1—4:13
   C. The Body of the Gospel, 4:14—24:53
      1. The Galilean Ministry of Jesus, 4:14—9:50
      2. Jesus' Travel to Jerusalem, 9:51—19:27
      3. Jesus in Jerusalem, 19:28—21:38
      4. The Passion Narrative, 22:1—23:56a
      5. The Resurrection Narrative, 23:56b—24:53
II. The Acts of the Apostles
   A. Prologue: the Mandate of the Risen Jesus, 1:1-26
   B. The Beginning in Jerusalem, 2:1—5:42
   C. The First Stage of the Mission, 6:1—9:31
   D. Antioch and the Beginning of the Gentile Mission, 9:32—15:35
   E. Paul's Mission in Asia Minor and Greece, 15:16—19:20
   F. Paul's Witness to the Gospel in Jerusalem and Rome, 19:21—28:31

Basic Themes of Luke and Acts

WE MUST TRACE SOME BASIC THEMES IN LUKE AND ACTS IN ORDER to place Acts' portrait of Paul in proper perspective. Luke sketches God's plan of salvation that moves from Israel to its fulfillment in Jesus' death and resurrection in Jerusalem, and which again moves out of Jerusalem to "the ends of the earth" (Acts 1:8)—to Rome, the center of the Roman Empire (Acts 28).

[3]Ibid., p. 289.

Luke's plan of salvation is marked by four prominent motifs: (a) continuity; (b) reliability; (c) divine guidance; and (d) from suffering to glory.

The motif of continuity is clearly announced in Luke's programmatic opening of his Gospel in 4:16-30. Here Luke rearranges Mark's opening statement: He omits Jesus' announcement, "The time is fulfilled, and the kingdom of God has come near" (Mark 1:14-15), and instead inserts Mark 6:1-6a in his programmatic opening-narrative (Luke 4:16-30). In Nazareth, Jesus announces that the time of fulfillment has come in him (4:16-21; cf. Isa. 61:1); predicts the Gentile mission of the church (Elijah sent to Sidon; Elisha to Syria [4:24-27]); and becomes the target of Israel's rejection—Israel refuses to be the Israel of God. It not only rejects the fulfillment of God's promise in Jesus, but also attempts to kill Jesus (4:28-30).

Thus, Luke's programmatic statement sketches the basic outline of God's plan of salvation in the Gospel and Acts: the Gospel is first offered to Israel (4:14—9:50), but Israel refuses to accept Jesus. The travel narrative (9:51—19:27), in expanding on the program of Luke 4:28 ("all in the synagogue were filled with rage") accentuates that Israel excludes itself from God's salvation in Jesus. So the climax of the travel narrative pronounces the final verdict on Israel: "But as for these enemies of mine who did not want me to be king over them—bring them here and slaughter them in my presence" (19:27; cf. also the characterization of Jerusalem as a city of violence which kills the prophets, 13:34-35).

Therefore, the gospel now goes out to the Gentiles. Luke 4:24-27 (see above) is elaborated in 14:15-24—The Parable of the Great Dinner—with its climactic ending: "I tell you, none of those who were invited will taste my dinner" (verse 24), and again in 24:46-47: "And he said to them, 'Thus it is written, that the Messiah is to suffer and to rise from the dead on the third day, and that repentance and forgiveness of sins is to be proclaimed in his name to all nations, beginning from Jerusalem.'"

Even more important is the fact that the program of Luke 4:16-30 centers on Jesus as the fulfillment of God's plan of salvation, as announced by Isaiah (Isa. 61:1; Luke 4:17-21). Indeed, since Jesus alone is the bearer of the Spirit in Luke, he alone can fulfill Isaiah 61:1 (4:18). Jesus' baptism (3:21-22) prepares him for his prophetic role in 4:18-21, because there the Spirit descends upon Jesus "in bodily form like a dove" (3:22; cf. also 4:1, 14).

It is crucial for Luke to portray Jesus as the center of salvation-history. The gospel is a saving event, inasmuch as its focus is on the words and works of Jesus, since they define forever the character of the kingdom of God. Jesus is not only the proclaimer of God's coming kingdom, but is himself the *autobasileia* (the kingdom itself). Thus Jesus announces that in his work and person the kingdom is present: "If it is by the finger of God that I cast out the demons, then the kingdom of God has come to you" (11:20; cf. 7:27; 10:9, 18).

The second motif Luke demonstrates is *the historical reliability* of God's plan of salvation. In his preface (1:1-4), he seems to blame his predecessors, the "many" (1:1) for having failed to narrate the gospel-tradition in an "orderly, continuous and accurate" way (1:3). And thus Luke wants to show the "solidity" of the gospel-tradition (1:4), that is, the historical accuracy of the saving facts of the gospel.

Therefore, Luke is the first evangelist to write a true "life of Jesus"—a biography, as it were, that attempts to connect the birth stories of Jesus with his childhood story (2:41-52) and subsequently with his ministry (3:23ff.) in a continuous narrative. In fact, our picture of the life of Jesus is mainly derived from Luke. And it is especially Jesus' humanity that dominates Luke's portrait: Jesus is the helper of the helpless; the friend of outcasts and of women; the healer of the sick; the advocate of the poor and the antagonist of the powerful and rich (cf., for instance, 6:20-26; 7:21-23; 15:1-2). What strikes us especially in Luke's narrative about Jesus is that even when Jesus himself is suffering and in need, he blesses and helps others (cf. his homily to the women on his way to the cross [23:28-31], and his words of comfort to the criminal who is crucified alongside of him: "Truly I tell you, today you will be with me in Paradise" [23:43]). Moreover, Luke accentuates the nobility of Jesus' death; thus, Jesus prays for God to forgive his murderers, surrenders his spirit to God, and evokes from the centurion the confession, "Certainly this man was innocent" (23:34, 46-47).

Luke's interest in the historical reliability of the gospel-tradition manifests itself in his emphasis on the historicity of the resurrection and ascension of Jesus. Luke alone among the Synoptic Gospel-writers portrays the physical return of the risen Jesus to his disciples: "Touch me and see; for a ghost does not have flesh and bones as you see that I have" (24:39). Again, Luke alone separates Jesus' resurrection from his ascension and inserts a forty-day sojourn of Jesus with his disciples between these events.

Luke's interest in historical reliability is also seen in his stressing the fact that when Jesus calls his twelve disciples he names them apostles (6:13). In contrast to Matthew and Mark where the term apostle rarely occurs (Matt. 10:2; Mark 3:14; 6:30), Luke regularly names the disciples apostles (6:13; 9:10; 11:49; 17:5; 22:14; 24:10). He does so in order to guarantee their reliable witness to both Jesus' ministry on earth and his resurrection (Acts 1:21-22). Luke's interest in the historicity of the gospel-tradition demands the equation of the twelve disciples with the twelve apostles. As a result, Paul, Luke's hero in Acts, does not qualify as an apostle, since he is dependent on the authority of the authentic apostles in Jerusalem (Acts 10:41; 13:31).

The third motif that marks Luke's conception of salvation-history centers on the notion of *divine guidance* and control. Robert Tannehill correctly points to the narrative unity of Luke-Acts: "Change and development are expected in such a narrative, yet unity is maintained because the scenes and characters contribute to a larger story that determines the significance of each part. . . . Luke-Acts is a unified narrative because the chief human characters (John the Baptist, Jesus, the apostles, Paul) share in a mission which expresses a single controlling purpose—the purpose of God."[4] Luke highlights God's plan in his narrative by frequently using phrases such as "the purpose of God" (*boulē tou theou* [Luke 7:30; Acts 2:23; 4:28; 5:38-39; 13:36; 20:27]); "the foreknowledge of God" (*prognōsis tou theou* [Acts 2:23]); and "it was necessary" (*dei* [Luke 9:22, 44; 17:25; 24:7, 26, 44; Acts 9:16; 14:22; 17:3; 19:21; 23:11; 27:24]). However, Luke never tells us why "it was necessary." Indeed, in his hands salvation-history has become something like a deterministic philosophy of history, dominated by the guidance of God and in accord with Scripture. Related to this motif of divine guidance is Luke's emphasis on Jesus' sovereign command over salvation-history: "He [Luke] wants to show that the passion is the realization of a divine plan that inaugurates the last days. Jesus is shown to be in charge of the passion events."[5] Thus, Jesus knows that the passion must be his destiny; the travel narrative (9:51—19:27) has Jerusalem and Jesus' forthcoming death continuously as its focus. Moreover, Jesus uses his passion as instruction for true discipleship (6:28; 23:34, 43).

The final motif in Luke's narrative can be paraphrased as *confusione hominum - Dei providentia* (where humans fail, God's providence rules). It comprises two aspects: one, from adversity to glory, and two, where humans fail, God corrects and directs. In other words, God brings good

---

[4]Robert C. Tannehill, *The Narrative Unity of Luke-Acts: A Literary Interpretation*, (Philadelphia: Fortress Press, 1986) 1. xiii.
[5]Powell, *What Are They Saying?* p.36.

out of evil, symbolized by the death and resurrection of Jesus, and it is later illustrated not only by the death of Stephen (Acts 7) — an event that leads to the mission of the Gentiles — but also by Paul's suffering in Jerusalem, a suffering that nevertheless brings the gospel to Rome.

Again, the story of Peter's refusal to eat non-kosher food leads to the conversion of Cornelius, the first gentile convert (Acts 10), and Paul's resolve to travel to Asia and Bithynia is thwarted by the Holy Spirit, so that Paul and Timothy cross over to missionize in Greece (Acts 16:6-10).

The Portrait of Paul in Acts

WHEN WE NOW TURN TO LUKE'S PORTRAIT OF PAUL IN ACTS, we must keep in mind that his description of Paul is embedded in his overall salvation-historical scheme. Just as Luke 4:16-30 forms the thematic preface to the Gospel, so Acts 1:6-8 functions as the theme of the Acts of the Apostles: "So when they had come together, they asked him, 'Lord, is this the time when you will restore the kingdom to Israel?' He replied, 'It is not for you to know the times or periods that the Father has set by his own authority. But you will receive power when the Holy Spirit has come upon you, and you will be my witnesses in Jerusalem, in all Judea and Samaria, and to the ends of the earth.' "

In the overarching context of God's sovereign will and plan that alone determine the worldwide outreach of the church, the mission "to the ends of the earth" refers unmistakably to Paul, since he almost single-handedly carries the gospel in ever-widening missionary conquests from Antioch (chapter 13) to Rome (chapter 28). There can be no doubt that Paul is the hero of Acts. In fact, it seems that the proper name for the Book of Acts should not be "the Acts of the Apostles," but rather "the Acts of Peter and Paul, especially those of Paul."

Although we hear about other apostles and missionaries in chapters 1–15, they all disappear from the scene: James, the brother of John, is killed by Herod Agrippa (12:2) and Peter, so prominent along with John in chapters 2–12, disappears suddenly and almost forever from the scene in chapter 12: "Then he left and went to another place" (12:17). Stephen, one of the seven Hellenists (6:1-6), is soon martyred (7:55-60) and we never hear again from the other Hellenists except for Philip, whose missionary activity in Samaria is described by Luke in 8:14-19 (see also 21:8: "We went into the house of Philip the evangelist, one of the seven"). And even Barnabas, Paul's companion on his missionary journeys, drops out of the picture when, after a quarrel with Paul over John Mark, he travels to Cyprus (15:37). Moreover, we do not hear again from James, the brother of the Lord and the president of the Jerusalem Church, after his presence at the Apostolic Council (chapter 15) until we meet him again briefly toward the end of the book (21:17-26).

Indeed, almost no other apostles and missionaries receive any attention, except Paul, who occupies center stage from chapter 13 to the end of Acts. Luke has introduced him to the reader in the narrative of the stoning of Stephen (7:58—8:1) and subsequently in the report of his violent persecution of the Christians (9:1-9), which leads to his sudden conversion and calling (9:10-19). In fact, the conversion story announces the theme that will characterize Paul's missionary activity throughout. Here the risen Lord tells Ananias: "He is an instrument whom I have chosen to bring my name before Gentiles and kings and before the people of Israel; I myself will show him how much he must suffer for the sake of my name" (9:15-16).

Indeed, from chapter 13 until the end of the book (chapter 28), Paul seems to be Luke's exclusive hero. One receives the impression that there were no fellow missionaries besides him, as if Paul alone was responsible for carrying the gospel "to the ends of the earth," according to Jesus' mandate to the apostles (1:8). Moreover, this mandate seems restricted to just the *Pauline* mission to the West—to Asia Minor, Greece, and Rome (cf. also 13:47, where Jesus' mandate of 1:8, now in the form of a citation from Isaiah 49:6, is applied to Paul alone). We may properly ask: Did not the gospel travel during this period to the Jewish diaspora in Babylonia and in East Asia (cf. Peter's mission to "the circumcision" in Gal. 2:7), as well as to North Africa, Illyria, and the Balkan; cf. Rom. 15:20)?

Moreover, in line with Luke's exclusive focus on Paul's mission, he must suppress two facts: one, he silences the presence of Christians in Rome prior to Paul's arrival there (Roman Jews are ignorant about the Christian sect [28:22], notwithstanding the fact that Christian brothers from Rome come to meet Paul [28:5]). And two, Luke ends his book on a victorious note, notwithstanding the fact that he knows about the death of Paul, which he foreshadows in several places (Agabus' prophecy in 21:11; cf. also Luke's final words at the time of Paul's departure from Miletus: "They would not see him again" [20:38]).

Luke portrays Paul's imprisonment in Rome as that of a man on parole who preaches the gospel "with all boldness and without hindrance" (28:31). Luke's intention is clear: He is a Gentile, his church—probably located somewhere in Asia Minor—owes its existence to Paul the missionary, who is now no longer available to the church. As a "chosen vessel" (9:15, KJV), Paul has executed God's saving purpose for the Gentiles. Luke wants to record this and therefore writes the Christian universal mission as Pauline mission. However, Luke does not engage in a hero worship of Paul, as if Paul's initiative and successes are his accomplishments. God—not Paul—is the basic initiator of the salvation of the Gentiles. Therefore, Luke writes the history of the church in a kerygmatic manner since he wants to demonstrate that the mission and expansion of the church are due solely to the providence of God. Indeed, God fulfills his promise to Israel in such a way that Gentiles can legitimately participate as "the true Israel" in God's saving history.

Conclusion

LUKE'S NARRATIVE, DOMINATED BY THE PLAN OF GOD AS ITS SINgle controlling purpose, unfolds its salvation-historical themes in Acts in terms of three interrelated subthemes: one, the theme of the unity of the church, which also prompts Luke's antiheretical stance; two, the theme of the political legitimacy of the church, which motivates Luke's pro-Roman attitude; and three, the theme of the theological legitimacy of the church, which stresses the continuity between the church and Israel. All three themes are designed to meet the problems that Luke's church faces at the end of the first century A.D.

The first theme portrays the church of the apostolic past as the *Una Sancta Apostolica*, which in its unity, harmony, and peace provides the model for Luke's own church. This idealized picture of the apostolic beginnings of the church, which is a mixture of historical memory and Luke's own literary purpose, emphasizes the purity and unity of the beginnings of the church and thus gives Luke a powerful weapon against heretics. For instance, Paul's farewell address to the elders of Ephesus in Miletus has a specific antiheretical focus:

> Keep watch over yourselves and over all the flock, of which the Holy Spirit has made you overseers (*episkopous*), to shepherd the church of God that he obtained with the blood of his own Son (*tou idiou*). I know that after I have gone (*meta tēn aphixin mou*), savage wolves will come in among you, not sparing the flock. Some even from your own group will come distorting the truth (*lalountes diestrammena*) in order to entice the disciples to follow them. Therefore be alert (*dio grēgoreite*), remembering that for

three years I did not cease night or day to warn everyone with tears (20:28-31).

Here Paul contemplates the future and addresses the danger Luke's church faces in the here and now. The heretical danger is twofold: There is a threat not only from "savage wolves" (verse 29) who will invade the church from the outside, but also from heretics who will arise within the church with their claim to present the gospel in a truer and more effective fashion.

And so Luke combats them by stressing the public, nonsecretive character of Paul's gospel (20:20) and his proclamation of "the whole purpose of God" (20:27). Although there are only a few references in Acts to the present threat of heresy (8:9-24; 20:28-31), Paul's farewell address in 20:17-35 demonstrates that Luke's antiheretical stance underscores not only the theme of the unity of the church, but also the theme of the continuity of tradition. Therefore, "Paul" emphasizes that the overseers (*episkopoi* [v. 28]), who are identical with the elders (*presbyteroi* [v. 17]) are charged with the leadership of Luke's church and must guard the continuity between past and present—between Paul's gospel and the present church.

The fact that Luke frames his speech of Paul as a farewell address underscores its importance because it carries all the weight of a last will and testament. In this context Roloff observes:

> The *Sitz im Leben* of the farewell discourse is the historical location of the institution or group, reflecting on the heritage which has been entrusted to it. The focus of interest is not so much the personal fate of the central figure of the past, but the historical effect of his work. The later generation begins to understand its own historical location when it realizes how much it has been shaped by its past heritage and is able to preserve this heritage for its own future.[6]

In short, the genre of the farewell discourse occupies an important function when historical continuity has become a problem, which in Luke's case means the continuity of the tradition from the second to the

---

[6]Jürgen Roloff, *Die Apostelgeschichte* (NTD 5; Göttingen: Vandenhoeck & Ruprecht, 1981) 302 (my translation).

third Christian generation. Indeed, Paul's farewell address occupies a unique place among the speeches of Acts: It is the only speech of Paul that is addressed to Christians and the only speech that is not a response to a specific urgent local problem. Moreover, it is the only speech in which the person of Paul himself is the focus and in which he presents to the church a synopsis of past, present, and future issues. Thus the speech emphasizes the continuity of tradition in the face of disruptive heresies.

The second theme that runs like a thread through Acts deals with the political legitimacy of the church. Luke's positive attitude toward the Roman Empire and its officials is remarkable, especially when it is compared with the radical stance of the Revelation to John against imperial Rome or with the more cautious disposition of the Pastoral Epistles. Indeed, Luke marks the beginning of the apologetic literature, which will flower in the second century A.D. For instance, Justin Martyr claims that Christians are the emperor's best allies in the cause of peace and good order (Apol. I, 11:1—12:1), while Tertullian posits Christianity as the soul of the empire (Apol. 1:25-33). Although Luke has a much more cautious attitude to the state than the Apologists and, moreover, addresses Christians and not Roman emperors, he intimates that when Christians behave properly they have nothing to fear from the state. The extent to which Luke articulates the political inoffensiveness of Christianity and its favorable reception by Roman officials is indeed surprising.

Just as the procurator Pilate pronounces Jesus innocent (and that three times, Luke 23:4, 14, 22), so the procurator Festus and King Agrippa declare Paul innocent of the charges of the Jews (26:32; see also 23:9; 24:16, 20; 25:8, 11, 25). Moreover, the proconsul of Achaia, Gallio, refuses to hear Jewish accusations against Paul (18:12-15), and a Roman centurion and tribunes guarantee Paul's safety during a riot in Jerusalem (21:27-36; 23:22) while another Roman centurion does not allow his soldiers to kill Paul during a shipwreck off Malta (27:43).

The favorable reaction of Roman officials to Paul is all the more surprising in the face of the continuous and politically effective accusations of the Jews: "These people [Paul and Silas] who have been turning the world upside down have come here also. . . . They are all acting contrary to the decrees of the emperor, saying that there is another king named Jesus" (17:6-7; cf. 16:21). Luke, like the apologists in the second century A.D., attempts with these pro-Roman features of his narrative to discredit the Roman charge of the subversive and revolutionary character of Christianity. Indeed, we must not forget that, in Luke's time, slander, ostracism, and the threat of persecution by Roman society were very real.

And these dangers were all the more acute because the church was considered to be no longer a Jewish sect, but an independent movement (the term *Christianos* occurs in the New Testament only three times — twice in Acts [11:26; 28:28] and once in 1 Peter [4:16]). In other words, Christians have now become a *tertium genus*, "a third race," and outsiders call them "Christians" instead of Jews (11:26). This means that the protection Judaism enjoyed in terms of what became later defined as *religio licita* (a protected religion under Roman law) is no longer theirs. Christians are now in danger of being outlawed as a *superstitio nova ac malefica*, a term used by Roman law to condemn new Oriental cults. Luke's pro-Roman attitude, then, is motivated by his attempt to protect the church against the threats of persecution, illegality, and social ostracism by the Roman state. In fact, this may well be one reason why Luke chooses not to narrate Paul's death at the hands of the Romans.

Luke's third theme focuses on the theological legitimacy of the church, which preoccupies him probably more deeply than the other themes. Although this issue is directly related to those of the unity of the church and of its political legitimacy, Luke's basic problem concerns the theological status of Christianity as a "third race" (*tertium genus*). For what will the status of this "third race" be now that it is no longer a part of either Judaism or pagan society? This problem has become all the more acute for the many recent gentile converts to Christianity who, as "God fearers" (*phoboumenoi; sebomenoi*), were formerly associated with the synagogue. For what does constitute henceforth their religious identity?

In other words, how can the church claim a legitimate identity when it professes a Jewish messiah as its Lord while the Jews themselves explicitly reject this "Christian" messiah? And how can the church claim to be "the true Israel" of God (see Luke 24:44) when it breaks down the very heart of Judaism — the covenant, the Torah, and circumcision? How can the church appropriate for itself the promises of the Jewish Scriptures and claim to present in Christ the fulfillment of God's covenant with Abraham when it has ostensibly separated itself from its parent religion by ceasing to be obedient to Israel's Torah? Moreover, this situation was exacerbated by the fact that the church had practically no success in converting Jews, notwithstanding its claims that the gospel primarily applies to them (2:38-42; see the emphasis on "first to you (Jews)" [3:26; 13:46]). And if Christianity is no longer committed to the Torah and to its Jewish heritage, how can it dismiss the Roman charge that it is simply another new mystery religion — a charge which, for instance, the Athenians level against Paul: "He [Paul] seems to be a proclaimer of foreign divinities (*xenōn daimoniōn*)"; "May we know what this new teaching is (*kainē di-dachē*) that you are presenting?" (17:18-19).

Luke now addresses the issue of the church's theological legitimacy by emphasizing the continuity of the church with Israel, that being the continuity of God's salvation-history. Therefore, his long section on "the trial of Paul" (chapters 21–28) is meant to demonstrate that Christianity is the fulfillment of Judaism rather than its abrogation. And so Luke points out that, whereas the rejection of the gospel by the Jews must be attributed to their ignorance and evil stubbornness (28:26-27), Paul himself stands squarely within the Jewish tradition (cf. 23:6; 24:14; 25:8; 26:1-8). In fact, these immoral Jewish traits have also led them to crucify their own messiah, Jesus (2:40; 3:17; 13:27; 17:30; see Luke 23:34). Therefore, the church is not a new mystery religion or a new philosophical sect (17:21), but instead constitutes the true people of God—the true Israel.

CHAPTER 12

The Gospel according to John

SOMETIMES IT IS HELPFUL TO VIEW A LITERARY COMPOSITION IN terms of a central image, which, although it has the danger of a caricature, symbolizes the intent of the writing involved. The Pauline letters are dominated by the Old Testament image of the prophetic *rib*: the lawsuit that God conducts against Israel and the nations. It suggests the imagery of a courtroom—of God's self-justification and victory in Christ over the evil powers that dominate his creation. Indeed, Paul's preference for judicial metaphors supports such a view.

When we survey the post-Pauline letter to the Ephesians, the image shifts from that of a courtroom to that of a liturgical festival in a Gothic cathedral. It is dominated, as I mentioned above, by a huge statue of *Christus Rex* on the reredos (the screen) above the altar. The festival's celebration focuses on Christ's cosmic victory in its significance for the church.

In a similar way, the Gospel of John has an imagery of its own, which may help us to discover the basic hermeneutical key to the Gospel. The Gospel of John presents a gospel-drama that resembles a medieval mystery play. The mystery of its dramatic character is that on stage there is a suspension of movement. Moreover, the stage is completely veiled in darkness except for a single focal light that shines on Jesus, who alone draws the light. He is the focus, in fact, of *all* light because he is the source of all light in a world suffocated by its own darkness. We may recall here the similarity between John and Rembrandt's etchings and paintings: the *chiaroscuro* used by the artist to make Jesus shine in the midst of darkness—the only subject matter of the canvas. In John, Jesus' words and actions are couched as monologues and soliloquies. The other voices and situations in John are nothing but stage props—occasions for Jesus' speech and action. They never cause the spotlight to move, because they come from the darkened part of the stage and recede again into the background once they have fulfilled their function of causing Jesus to speak and to move the narrative along.

For instance, in John 12:21, some Greeks appear on the scene who say to Philip, "We wish to see Jesus." But instead of addressing them personally, Jesus makes a symbolic speech about his hour of glorification (12:23-36). Similarly, in chapter 3, Nicodemus functions as a stage prop, prompting Jesus to speak about rebirth (3:3). In chapter 4 the Samaritan woman has the same function when she asks, "How is it that you, a Jew, ask a drink of me, a woman of Samaria?" prompting Jesus to speak about the water of eternal life (4:9-26). Misunderstandings by the stage props cause Jesus to speak about the true mystery that he himself is. Moreover, they anticipate the solution of the mystery, which will be disclosed at the time of Jesus' impending death and exaltation. This is clear in passages like 13:36, "Simon Peter said to him, 'Lord, where are you going?'"; 14:8, "Philip said to him, 'Lord, show us the Father and we will be satisfied' "; and 16:17-18, "Some of his disciples said to one another, 'What does he mean by saying to us, "A little while, and you will no longer see me, and again a little while and you will see me," and "Because I am going to the Father"?' They said, 'What does he mean by this " little while"? We do not know what he is talking about.' "

The scenario of stage props—of repeated misunderstandings and queries seem to come to an end at 16:29: "His disciples said, 'Yes, now you are speaking plainly, not in any figure of speech!' " However, soon thereafter, in 16:31-35, Jesus' prediction of the disciples' betrayal shows that the final resolution of their misunderstanding does not come until Jesus' passion and exaltation (chapters 18–20).

Although there is some external movement toward the passion and exaltation of Jesus and some internal movement toward greater degrees of faith and understanding by the disciples, from another perspective there is practically no action or movement in the Gospel. There is hardly a plot offered to us or a reversal scene, or even a true resolution or catharsis. We know the plot from the start, and it recurs in every scene, so that, when the action finally climaxes in the passion narrative in chapters 18–20, it seems merely a fitting conclusion and closure to all the preceding scenes.

Indeed, the prologue of 1:1-18 is actually a summary of the whole Gospel, for even here the Passion is foreshadowed: "He came to what was his own, and his own people did not accept him" (1:11). And, lest we forget, the frequent "remembering" clauses must remind us of the meaning of the passion and exaltation. For instance, in 2:22 where Jesus speaks about the temple of his body, the text comments: "After he was raised from the dead, his disciples remembered that he had said this." And again in 12:16, at the time of Jesus' entry into Jerusalem, we read: "His disciples did not understand these things at first; but when Jesus was glorified, then they remembered that these things had been written of him and had been done to him" (cf. also 2:17).

The clauses "not yet" (*oupō*; cf. 2:4; 7:6, 8, 30, 39; 8:20; 20:17) and "no longer" (*ouketi*; cf. 4:42; 6:66; 11:54; 14:19, 30; 10:10, 16, 25; 17:11) suggest progress and movement, and yet they seem to function only as dramatic devices that must give the narrative its character of suspense, although they are actually retrospective reflections, that is, reflections from the perspective of the closure point of the drama, which occurs at Easter (chapter 20). For it is only at Easter that when the Spirit descends on the disciples, they are able to understand and remember the true meaning of Jesus' words and actions (cf. 20:22: "Jesus breathed on them and said to them, 'Receive the Holy Spirit.' "). Indeed, the Gospel stresses that while before Easter, Jesus alone possesses the Spirit (1:32-33; 3:34), he promises the disciples this gift of the Spirit/*Paraklete* (Counselor) after his departure (7:39; 14:15-17; 14:25-26; 15:26-27; 16:4-15).

The Gospel of John is indeed as dramatic as one of Rembrandt's *chiaroscuro* paintings: The mysterious spotlight falls exclusively on Jesus and everything else is only present as a foil to highlight his divine radiance. John gives us, in Paul Tillich's words, "a picture" of the Christ: the New Being in the midst of transient existence.[1] It is almost a static picture. The basic movement seems to occur only in the beholding eye and in the response of the observer. Indeed, the Gospel asks us only one essential question: Do you or do you not see in this picture the transparency of the divine in the human face of Jesus, and in seeing it, are you transformed by the divine glory that has descended from heaven to embrace you and take you up into its radiance? And so throughout the Gospel the emphasis is on the themes of life, light, glory, and on those of seeing/beholding, and thus, on knowing from within.

---

[1] Paul Tillich, *Systematic Theology*, vol. 2 (Chicago: University of Chicago Press, 1957) 2. 97–98.

How different all this is from the portrait of Jesus in the Synoptic Gospels! Matthew portrays Jesus as the Messiah of Israel, who is not only the healing Messiah, but also the teaching Messiah and the suffering Messiah. As healing Messiah he is the Lord of divine power (cf. the miracle stories); as teaching Messiah he gives his disciples a new Torah from a new Mount Sinai, and is embroiled in discussions about Jewish oral law, while his promise of life focuses on heeding his commandments. And finally, as suffering Messiah he sheds his blood "for the forgiveness of sins" (26:28) at his crucifixion (27:38-54).

Luke, again, portrays Jesus quite differently from John. Here, we encounter the humane Jesus—friend of the poor, outcasts, and women—who draws us by his compassion and acts of mercy. His preaching of the kingdom of God evokes the hostility of his Jewish adversaries, and he dies as a righteous, suffering martyr, as the symbol of crucified innocence.

Much closer to John's portrayal of Jesus than either Matthew's or Luke's is Mark's rendering. Both Mark and John emphasize the mystery of Jesus and the profound misunderstanding of even his closest disciples—a misunderstanding that only Jesus' passion and resurrection can remove (cf. Mark 4:11; 14:28; 16:6-7). And yet, how different is the historical portrait of Jesus in Mark from the symbolic portrait of Jesus in John! In Mark there is a real struggle about Jesus' true identity. Who is he—an impressive miracle worker or God's suffering Messiah? The messianic secret in Mark functions to heighten the tension around Jesus' mysterious identity: How can he be so publicly engaged and yet not want to be known as the Son of God? And even when Jesus makes his public confession in 14:62, how do we assess his dying on the cross and especially his cry, "My God, my God, why have you forsaken me?" (15:34).

Is Jesus' glory only known in his death and suffering? Indeed, the confession of the centurion at the foot of the cross seems to indicate this: "Now when the centurion, who stood facing him, saw that in this way he breathed his last, he said, 'Truly this man was God's son' " (Mark 15:39). The centurion is portrayed as a true disciple because he acknowledges Jesus as God's son before his resurrection.

All this is absent in John. Indeed, a cry of dereliction on the cross does not fit John's portrait of Jesus. Instead, Jesus speaks from the cross, "It is finished" (19:30), as if he realizes that he has come to the end of his appointed itinerary. In fact, in contrast to Mark, Jesus' identity in the Gospel of John is, however mysterious, clear from the outset. He is the one who is God's only begotten son, who exclaims "the Father and I are one," as the Gospel climactically states in 10:30.

No messianic secret surrounds the Johannine Jesus. He proclaims publicly and openly his unique relation to God. Moreover, that is basically all he proclaims: "Believe the works [I do] so you may know and understand that the Father is in me and I am in the Father" (10:38). The subject matter of the proclamation is the proclaimer himself. The Johannine Jesus displays his identity publicly; it is not slowly arrived at in a process of increasing messianic consciousness, whether at his baptism (Mark 1:9-11), at Caesarea Philippi (Mark 8:27-30), or at the glorification on the Mount (Mark 9:2-13). In John, Jesus' identity is his own from all eternity. Therefore, there is no scene of a private epiphany to Jesus on the Mount of Glorification followed by a command to silence to the three disciples who accompany him (Mark 9:2-13). Instead, a public manifestation of Jesus' glory before the crowd is substituted for it in John 12:28-30.

Likewise, John omits the Gethsemane scene of the Synoptic Gospels and strikes all references to Jesus' struggles and temptations. In fact, where the Synoptic Gospels describe Jesus' suffering in Gethsemane and his cry of dereliction, John 12—the chapter that introduces Jesus' Farewell Discourses (13—16)—reports his oneness with his Father's purpose and states that the heavenly voice that glorifies him does not occur for the sake of Jesus, but rather for the sake of the crowd (12:27-33). Thus, the moment of Jesus' death and humiliation is interpreted as the moment of victory and exaltation: "Now is the judgment of this world, now the ruler of this world will be driven out" (12:31). Indeed, the Johannine Jesus is so at one with the Father that he does not need to pray for himself, but only prays for the sake of the people at the event of the raising of Lazarus (11:41-42).

And so the Rembrandt painting of the Johannine Jesus is quite appropriate. Because the Markan Jesus participates both in the light and in the darkness, he does not emerge into the full light until the events of his death and resurrection. However, the Johannine Jesus stands in the full light from the beginning of time, and even the cross cannot dim the light, because it is an integral element in Christ's moment of glorification. Indeed, the "lifting up" of Jesus on the cross coincides with his being "lifted up" into heaven (12:32-34; cf. 3:14; 8:28-29).

Jesus, then, in the Gospel of John is an artistic object rather than a historical figure, someone who is engaged in working out his identity. Indeed, the dramatic, historical Jesus of Mark is here displaced by an on-

tologically static Jesus. The light of the resurrection has here so perme-
ated the figure of Jesus that his historical life from birth to the cross is
eclipsed by his preexistence and his post-existence—the heavenly descent
of his incarnation and the heavenly ascent into his exaltation. The dual
movements of descent and ascent determine in John the basic interpretation of Jesus. Therefore, the criterion of faith is whether we acknowledge
the heavenly descent and ascent of Jesus as God's "only Son" (1:14).

In fact, in John the light of the resurrection fuses so much with that
of the incarnation that it threatens to wipe out the human features of
Jesus. Notwithstanding the proclamation, "the Word became flesh and
lived among us" (1:14), Jesus is a Jesus of public glory (*doxa*), rather than
a Jesus of hidden glory (*krypsis*) as in Mark, or a fully humane Jesus as in
Luke.

John's Christology "from above," that is, of divine incarnation, has
completely obscured a Christology "from below," a Christology that
centers on the resurrection as the moment when Jesus receives the status
of God's son (cf. Rom. 1:4; Acts 2:22-24, 32–33, 36).

As I mentioned above, Paul Tillich centers his Christology on the
picture of Jesus as the Christ. It is a picture of Christ as the One, in whom
the New Being is manifest. For Tillich, Jesus is the Christ inasmuch as
the New Being is victoriously present under the conditions of existence,
estrangement, and alienation. Tillich's picture of Jesus as the Christ is
indeed quite close to the Johannine Jesus. Indeed, the only thing that matters for John is whether we do or do not see God's presence in the human
face of Jesus. The prologue to the Gospel states emphatically, "*We* have
seen his glory, the glory as of a Father's only Son, full of grace and truth"
(1:14b).

In this context, we must be aware of how crucial and intricate John's
terminology of faith is. *Believing, seeing,* and *knowing* form a triadic complex. True faith involves both believing and knowing as, for example, in
6:68, "Simon Peter answered him, 'Lord, to whom shall we go? You
have the words of eternal life. We have come to *believe* and *know* that you
are the Holy One of God.' " Moreover, *believing* and *knowing* culminate
in a type of seeing: "We have *seen* his glory, the glory as of a father's only
son " (1:14b) and "Many of the Jews therefore, who had come with Mary
and had *seen* what Jesus did, *believed* in him" (11:45).

True faith is determined by a person's attitude toward the signs Jesus
performs. Faith remains ambiguous—if not false—if it misunderstands
the true significance of the signs. When faith is purely directed to Jesus'
miraculous works, that is, to the signs he performs (2:23f.; 11:45), or to

Jesus' material gifts (6:26), it is not true faith. For real faith perceives that the true signs are Jesus' death and resurrection, his being lifted up on the cross. Otherwise, the signs induce false faith: "Unless you see signs and wonders you will not believe" (4:48; cf. 6:2, 14).

Indeed, in the Johannine gospel-drama all fingers point to the light on center stage, which is Jesus. And the basic question that Jesus asks of us is whether we are able to discern in him the Word that became flesh and lived among us (1:14). And our answer to that question depends on whether the face of Jesus becomes for us an icon which, however human, is illuminated by a mysterious divine presence. Indeed, in John faith is illuminated faith—a type of faith that is simultaneously a seeing and knowing faith. For the law of the Spirit in John dictates that "only like knows like": only the enlightened (*illuminati*) can behold the light (*lumen*) of the glory of Jesus (1:14; cf. 1 John 1:1).

The Johannine community is a group of the spiritually endowed (pneumatics): "When the Spirit of Truth comes, he will guide you into all the truth" (16:13). It is the *Paraklete* (the Advocate) who, as Jesus promises, "will be with you forever. This is the Spirit of truth, whom the world cannot receive, because it neither sees him nor knows him. You know him, because he abides with you, and he will be in you" (14:16-17).

The controlling images for John's Gospel are both a Rembrandtesque Christ and a Greek Orthodox icon, in which divinity permeates humanity. This not only characterizes Christ, but will also be our destiny. As the Gospel states in 11:26, "Everyone who lives and believes in me will never die" and as the first epistle of John says so poignantly: "We know that when he appears, we shall be like him" (1 John 3:2).

CHAPTER 13

The Epistle to the Hebrews

LUKE JOHNSON OPENS HIS COMMENTS ON HEBREWS IN THIS WAY: "For a writing of such beauty and power, Hebrews goes largely unread by ordinary Christians who are nourished by John and Paul."[1] He attributes as reasons for this neglect the sustained argument that the letter must be read completely from beginning to end and the complex symbolization of the ancient world that is alien to our own.

Hebrews presents itself as "a word of exhortation" (*paraklēsis*, 13:22; cf. 6:18; 12:5), a term that connotes both encouragement (6:18) and warning (12:5). Although Hebrews has an epistolary ending (13:22-25), it is a homily in which exposition and exhortation alternate. Didactic arguments, mostly based on a typological interpretation of the Old Testament law, are followed throughout by warnings and exhortations to the readers.[2]

The Outline of the Epistle

THE OUTLINE OF THE EPISTLE DEMONSTRATES THIS ALTERNATION between exposition and exhortation:

    A. Exposition, 1:1-14

---

[1]Luke T. Johnson, *The Writings of the New Testament: An Interpretation* (Philadelphia: Fortress Press, 1986) 412.
[2]Notice, for example, the frequent use of clauses that mark the transition from exposition to exhortation: "therefore" (*dio*, 3:7, 9; 6:1; 12:12, 28); "thus" (*oun*, 4:1, 11, 14, 16; 10:19, 35; cf. also 2:1; 3:1; 12:1; 13:13).

B. Exhortation, 2:1-4
C. Exposition, 2:5—3:6a
D. Exhortation, 3:6b—4:16
E. Exposition, 5:1-10
F. Exhortation, 5:11—6:20
G. The Central Exposition, 7:1—10:18
    1. Christ, the high priest, after the order of Melchizedek, 7:1-28
    2. The eschatological perfection of Christ, the high priest, 8:1—9:28
    3. The eschatological efficacy of Christ and his high priestly work, 10:1-18
H. Exhortation,[3] 10:19—13:25

The Two Themes of the Epistle

ALTHOUGH LUKE JOHNSON STATES THAT HEBREWS CONTAINS ONE sustained argument from beginning to end,[4] there seem to be present two basic themes in the epistle that are difficult to integrate with each other.

The first theme deals with the priestly work of Christ who, in his "once-for-all" sacrifice (*ephapax*, 7:27; 9:12; 10:10), has sanctified and perfected forever, "those who approach God through him" (7:25). In other words, this theme, which 7:1—10:18 elaborates, emphasizes the finality and all-sufficiency of Christ's sacrifice.

The second theme is devoted to the people of God as a pilgrimage people. Here, Christ is cast not as the high priest, but as the pilgrim-pioneer: "Looking to Jesus the pioneer and perfecter of our faith, who for the sake of the joy that was set before him endured the cross disregarding its shame, and has taken his seat at the right hand of the throne of God" (12:2). Jesus is here the forerunner and pioneer (2:10) of our salvation, and our salvation depends on running "with perseverance the race that is set before us" (12:1). This race is as serious and as full of pitfalls as the pilgrimage of the Exodus-generation under Moses—those people who "hardened their hearts" (3:8, 15; 4:7) and were not allowed to enter God's rest (3:11, 18). Therefore, the Christian readers are admonished, "Let us therefore make every effort to enter that rest, so that no one may fall through such disobedience as theirs" (4:11).

---

[3]The exhortation "therefore" is almost totally absent in 7:1—10:18, but reappears in 10:19-35.
[4]Johnson, *The Writings of the New Testament,* p. 412.

Thus, there seem to be two disparate themes in Hebrews: whereas the motif of Christ, the all-sufficient high priest dominates in 7:1 — 10:18, the Exodus motif of pilgrimage is the central focus of 3:7 — 4:13 and of 11:1 — 13:25.[5] Moreover, the problem of integrating the two themes is made more acute when we observe the difference between two symbolisms that Hebrews employs. On the one hand, we encounter the symbolism of a temple scene, the holy of holies, where Christ the high priest sheds his blood and sacrifices himself for the expiation of sins. Here a *vertical-static* imagery of a temple-service suggests itself. It highlights Jesus' relation to both God and us in his role as mediator and perfect sacrifice, a sacrifice far superior to the one ordained by Old Testament law.

On the other hand, a *horizontal-dynamic* imagery prevails. It focuses on believers as the New Israel, the new people of God who are called to be a pilgrimage people. As such, they continue God's mandate to the Israel of old to be a people who marches through the wilderness of this transient world without any visible securities and possessing solely the promise of God, to whom they are called to be faithful (4:1-2, 11; 6:12; 10:23; 11:11). In fact, within the New Testament, it is only Hebrews that defines God as "the promising one" (*ho epangeilamenos*, 10:23; 11:11). Furthermore, the integration of the two themes is made all the more difficult because of the different connotations of the notion of faith and its object. It is striking first of all that "faith" (*pistis*) occurs in Hebrews more than in any other New Testament writing (32 times; 24 times in chapter 11 alone!); and secondly that the term is absent in the central high priestly sections of 7:1 — 10:18 and that it is mainly present in the pilgrimage and exhortation chapters.[6] Moreover, "faith" is nowhere defined as a term of salvation (soteriological term) with Christ as its object, but rather is used in an absolute sense as an ethical term. (God is the object of faith in 6:1 and 11:6.)

Thus, in Hebrews, "faith" means primarily the attitude of unwavering steadfastness and perseverance; it is synonymous with endurance and trust in the promise of God (cf. especially 10:23; 11:11). Faith, therefore, in Hebrews is inseparable from the "hope" of the believer: "We want each one of you to show the same diligence so as to realize the full assur-

---

[5]It is interesting in this respect that Käsemann entitles his commentary on Hebrews *The Wandering People of God*, trans. R. A. Harrisville and I. L. Sandberg (Minneapolis: Augsburg Press, 1984).
[6]The exceptions are 6:1; 10:22, 38 (Habekkuk 2:4), 39.

ance of hope to the very end, so that you may not become sluggish, but imitatiors of those who through faith and patience inherit the promises" (6:11-12; cf. also 6:18-19; 7:19; 11:11). The relation of God's promise to the hope of the believer is especially clear in 10:23 and 11:11 where, in both cases, God is defined as the one who is faithful to his promise (*pistos gar ho epangeilamenos*) and thus constitutes the foundation of the believer's hope: "Let us hold fast to the confession of our hope without wavering, for he who has promised is faithful" (10:23; cf. 11:11).

In this context, we must be aware that the two symbolisms (see above) evoke a different understanding of faith. With the symbolism of Christ as the high priest, faith connotes a momentous decision (10:38-39) to what Christ has accomplished "once for all" (7:27; 9:26; cf. 9:12; 10:10). In other words, here faith is believing assent to an accomplished fact and thus is a saving faith (10:39). In addition, this conception of faith as commitment to the "once-for-all" act of Christ points to a realized eschatology, that is, to the finality of our redemption. Thus, 9:12 states that Christ "obtains for us an eternal redemption," so that "by God's will . . . we have been sanctified through the offering of the body of Jesus Christ once for all" (10:10). In stressing the finality, the "once-for-all" character of Christ's sacrifice, the author intends to heighten the contrast to the incomplete sacrificial regulations of the Old Testament law: "If the worshipers [of the Old Testament covenant] had once been cleansed, they would no longer have any consciousness of sin" (10:2, *RSV*). Indeed, 2:11 proclaims an ontological unity between Christ and the believers, "for the one who sanctifies and those who are sanctified all have one Father."

However, the connotation of faith is quite different in the pilgrim symbolism of Hebrews. Since faith is here not assent to the accomplished act of Christ, but rather — as we have seen — trust in and reliance on God's promise, it actualizes itself as endurance amidst testing and hardships. And this persevering trust looks forward "to the city that has foundations, whose architect and builder is God" (11:10). In this vein, the author concludes his exhortation to pilgrimage: "Therefore, since we are surrounded by so great a crowd of witnesses, let us also [like the Old Testament believers of old] lay aside every weight and the sin that clings so closely, and let us run with perseverance the race that is set before us" (12:1).

Finally, the two basic themes of Hebrews clash in their interpretations of the Old Testament. Whereas within the pilgrimage sections there is a basic continuity between the Old Testament and the gospel, so that the Old Testament has a valid claim on the faithful of the Old Testament and on Christian believers alike (cf. especially chapter 11), within the high priestly chapters this continuity is displaced by a sharp discontinuity. For here the Old Testament law is only a "shadow" of the gospel and as such, it is an "obsolete" reality (8:13; 10:8-9).

The Contingent Situation of the Readers

Now that we have exposed the incongruities between the two basic themes of Hebrews, the question arises if there can nevertheless be found an interrelation between these themes that would sustain Luke Johnson's claim that Hebrews contains one sustained argument (see above). If that were the case, it would establish for Hebrews a basic coherent structure. However, before this task can be undertaken, we must discover whether there is a clear, contingent aspect in Hebrews that would make the epistle conform to what I earlier argued is characteristic of the New Testament writings—the interaction between coherence and contingency (cf. especially my treatment of the letters of Paul).

At this point, another difficulty arises. For just as it is a problem to delineate the basic coherence of Hebrews, so it has been likewise a problem for scholarship to discover the contingency of the epistle. We simply do not know who the author is, who his audience is, or where it is located. Moreover, we only know, in general terms, their social situation and religious conflicts.

Also, Hebrews manifests a certain rhetorical abstractness. So Luke Johnson states: "The literary artistry of the writer gives us pause, for an accomplished rhetorician need not rely on the condition of his hearers for the generation of themes. Some may derive simply from his imagination, others from the literary inertia created by his primary themes."[7] This proposal flies in the face of the very character of all New Testament writings. Surely, the author of Hebrews is not a fictitious writer who, like the Stoic Seneca, simply pens meditations for himself. It is one thing to confess that we modern interpreters are unable to determine the exact target of the author, but it is quite another matter to attribute to our author an abstract, imaginative piece of writing, however aesthetic it may be. If such were the case, the word of the gospel would disintegrate from "a word on target" to a literary essay without contact with a particular audience and thus cease to be gospel. After all, the epistle shows that there

---

[7]Johnson, *The Writings of the New Testament,* p. 415.

is physical dispossession and suffering among its readers (10:32-35; 12:3-13; 13:13-14). Moreover, the author issues repeated warnings about spiritual temptations (2:18), despair, and discouragement (2:12; 5:11; 12:16-17).

Indeed, the contingent situation of the readers may not be as obscure as many scholars think. The "word of exhortation," with which the epistle closes (13:22) and which — as we have seen — denotes both "warning" and "encouragement," suggests a twofold danger for the community. In the first place, the community, made up of former Jews and Godfearers (Gentiles attached to the synagogue), faces the temptation of sliding back into a form of Judaism. Therefore, the author emphasizes the absoluteness and finality of Christ's sacrifice, which does not tolerate a return to the "obsolete" cultic ordinances of the Old Testament or to any form of angel worship (1:4—2:9; 8:13; 9:1-26). Second, the temptation to slide back into Judaism is all the more attractive because of the persecution Christians face from the Roman Empire. After all, since Judaism had the status of a *religio licita* (an approved religion) under Roman law, a return to Judaism would provide Christians not only with a familiar religious home, but also with security within the Empire. It may well be that, as the postscript, "Those from Italy send you greetings" (13:24) indicates the community is in Rome[8] and has endured the persecution under the emperor Nero (54–68 A.D.) in the past (10:32-34), while it is now threatened with a new persecution under the emperor Domitian (81–96 A.D.).

The Integration of the Themes

WE MUST NOW REOPEN THE QUESTION OF WHETHER Hebrews possesses a basic coherence-contingency pattern. If, as we have tried to show, the epistle discloses a clear contingent dimension, can we claim the same for its coherent structure? In other words, is it possible to discover a theological integration between the two seemingly disparate themes that I outlined above?

Indeed, the author's conception of Christ (his Christology) may well provide the key to a solution of the problem. In order to discern this, we must pay attention to what for the author is one long, sustained argument.

———————————

[8]This would explain that 1 Clement, written from Rome (96 A.D.), is the earliest document that cites Hebrews frequently.

In his introduction (4:14—6:20) to the high priest section of 7:1—10:18, he intends to correlate the two seemingly disparate themes of Christ as the high priest and as the forerunner of the pilgrimage people. Thus, within his introductory comments to this theme (cf. especially 5:11-14), he combines concepts central to the Exodus theme with those that belong to the high priest theme. For example, 6:19-20, "We have this *hope*, a sure and steadfast anchor of the soul, a *hope* that enters *the inner shrine behind the curtain*, where Jesus, a *forerunner* on our behalf, has entered, having become *a high priest forever according to the order of Melchizedek*" (cf. also 6:9-18; 7:19).

The composition of the epistle shows an alternating sequence of exposition and exhortation (see above). This scheme conforms closely to what we call in the letters of the New Testament the relation of indicative (the gift of salvation in the gospel) and imperative (the demand to act in accordance with the gospel). For instance, we have seen that the letters of Paul manifest a composition in which the doctrinal section is regularly followed by an ethical section. The author of Hebrews follows a similar composition except that he alternates throughout his epistle the "indicative" (expository) and "imperative" (exhortatory) sections, whereas Paul in his letters does so in sequential blocks (cf., for example, Gal. 1–4 [doctrinal]; Gal. 5–6 [ethical]; Rom. 1–11 [doctrinal]; Rom. 12–15 [ethical]).

Thus, the author of Hebrews focuses in the high priestly sections on the "indicative"—the ground of our salvation, and in the pilgrimage sections on the "imperative"—the ethical mandates of the gospel. In other words, notwithstanding the different symbolisms and the different connotations of faith that I have outlined above, the author's basic intent is to show that the pilgrimage of believers is made hopeful and reliable because of what Christ as our high priest has made possible in his sacrifice "once for all." The Christian life of pilgrimage (3:7—4:13; 11:1—13:25), then, is engendered by what Christ has accomplished for us (cf. the central section of 7:1—10:18).

It is especially the author's conception of Christ that enables him to conjoin the two themes of Christ, the high priest and Christ, the forerunner, pioneer, and perfecter of our faith (2:10; 6:20; 12:2). One could argue that Hebrews is on the way to the Christology of Chalcedon (451 A.D.), where the nature of Christ was defined as perfectly human and perfectly divine. As Luke Johnson states: "Because Jesus is priest, the Christology of Hebrews must be both 'high' and 'low.' To offer a truly efficacious sacrifice, Jesus must be the eternal Word, the true Son of God, living 'by the power of an indestructible life' (7:16). But to be an effective mediator, he must be fully human as well."[9] Indeed, the function of Christ as high priest and Son of God makes it necessary that he combines in himself both divine and human attributes.

The Humanity of Jesus

ONE OF THE MOST IMPRESSIVE FEATURES OF HEBREWS IS THE POR-trayal of Jesus' humanity. No other writing of the New Testament — not even the Synoptic Gospels in their passion stories — portrays the depth of the human life of Jesus in the way this author does. O. Cullmann, the famous Swiss biblical scholar, writes: "The author of Hebrews — as per-haps no other early Christian theologian — had the courage to speak of the man Jesus in shockingly human terms — although he emphasized per-haps more strongly than any other the deity of the Son."[10] This is espe-cially clear in the following passages:

> Since, therefore, the children share flesh and blood, he himself likewise shared the same things, so that through death he might destroy the one who had the power of death, that is, the devil, and free those who all their lives were held in slavery by the fear of death. . . . Therefore, he had to become like his brothers and sisters in every respect, so that he might be a merciful and faith-ful high priest in the service of God, to make a sacrifice of atone-ment for the sins of the people. Because he himself was tested by what he suffered, he is able to help those who are being tested (2:14-18).

And again:

> In the days of his flesh, Jesus offered up prayers and supplica-tions, with loud cries and tears, to the one who was able to save him from death, and *he was heard in his fear* [see note 12, below]. Although he was a Son, he learned obedience through what he suffered, and having been made perfect, he became the source of eternal salvation to all who obey him, having been designated by

---

[9]Johnson, *The Writings of the New Testament*, p.426.
[10]Oscar Cullmann, *The Christology of the New Testament*, trans. S. C. Guthrie & C. A. M. Hall (rev. ed.; Philadelphia: Westminster Press, 1963) 93.

God a high priest according to the order of Melchizedek (5:7-10; my translation).

In particular, the author emphasizes four aspects of the human life of Jesus:

1) The *particularity* of Jesus' human life. He uses the simple name of Jesus as a title nine times (2:9; 3:1; 4:14; 6:20; 7:22; 10:19; 12:24; 13:12, 20).

2) The depth of *Jesus' temptation* (2:18). Cullmann comments:

> The fact that Jesus was tempted is a definite element of the gospel-tradition. But whereas in the Synoptics Jesus never even lets temptation approach him (except possibly at Gethsemane), *Hebrews* presupposes even more strongly the possibility of his sinning precisely by mentioning it together with his sinlessness. . . . And so we may ask along with H. Windisch: "Can we really assert in the strictest sense the sinlessness of one who was attracted by temptations exactly as we are?"[11]

3) The notion of *Jesus' weakness*, made manifest in his susceptibility to temptation (2:18) dominates 5:7-10 also, especially Jesus' fear in Gethsemane, where verse 7b could be rendered: "He was heard in his fear (anxiety)."[12] "To the scene in Gethsemane, as we know it from the Gospels, *Hebrews* adds that in his fear of death Jesus cried aloud and wept."[13]

4) The phrase "he learned obedience" presupposes an inner *human development*. "The life of Jesus would not be really human if its course did not manifest a development. In other words, *Hebrews* is not so much interested in Jesus *becoming* man as in his *being* man."[14]

Conclusion

Notwithstanding my earlier reservations (see above), the twin motifs in Hebrews — high priest and Exodus — are profoundly linked. Indeed, the

---

[11]Ibid. p. 89.
[12]According to Cullmann, Héring, and Windisch. I reject the *NRSV* translation: ". . . because of his reverent submission."
[13]Cullmann, *The Christology of the New Testament*, p. 96.
[14]Ibid., p. 97.

gift and demand of salvation are both symbolized in the twofold nature of Christ, so that the person of Christ himself becomes a paradigm for the basis of Christian life. For Christ represents in his work as high priest the joyful finality of our salvation, whereas his humanity with its pitfalls and temptations represents the call to ethical obedience and perseverance.

Therefore, the author of Hebrews exhorts his audience in the final chapter with the following words: "Jesus suffered outside the city gate in order to sanctify the people by his own blood. Let us then go to him outside the camp and bear the abuse he endured. For here we have no lasting city, but we are looking for the city that is to come" (13:12-14).

Hebrews issues a challenge to us: Bearing abuse for the sake of Jesus in order to gain true life means to live as a pilgrim in the world, just as Abraham "looked forward to the city that has foundations, whose architect and builder is God" (11:10), and therefore "stayed for a time in the land he had been promised, as in a foreign land, living in tents. . . ." (11:9) Indeed, it means to forsake our routinized securities and worldly advantages. For living in the world "as in a foreign land" carries the promise of an eternal blessing, which Christ, our high priest, has secured for us.

CHAPTER 14

The First Letter of Peter

WE NOW TURN TO THE SO-CALLED CATHOLIC EPISTLES: 1 PETER, 2 Peter, 1 John, 2 John, 3 John, Jude, and James. Although 1 Peter is the only Catholic Epistle that I discuss in this book, it is certainly one of the most important documents not only among the Catholic Epistles, but within the New Testament as a whole. The prescript of the letter shows its "catholic" character: ". . . to the exiles of the Dispersion in Pontus, Galatia, Cappadocia, Asia, and Bithynia" (1:1). Indeed, 1 Peter, like Ephesians, is an encyclical letter.

I adopt here a procedure that differs in some respects from the previous chapters. I shall conduct a hermeneutical probe that focuses on the issue of suffering and hope. Thus I will not discuss the many literary and historical problems that 1 Peter presents, such as the question of its unity or its pseudepigraphical character.

Outline of the Letter

A. Prescript, 1:1-2
B. Part I. Christian Salvation and the Duties of Christians, 1:3—4:11
  1. Election and Sanctification, 1:3—2:10
    a. Eulogy, 1:3-12
    b. Christianity as Sanctification, 1:13-21
    c. Christians as Children of God and as Mutual Brothers and Sisters, 1:22—2:10
  2. Paraenesis/Exhortation, 2:11—4:11

The Nature of Suffering and Hope

THE THEME OF 1 PETER IS SUFFERING. NO OTHER BOOK IN THE New Testament uses the verb "to suffer" (*paschō*) and the noun "suffering" (*pathēma*) as frequently (the verb occurs in 2:19, 20, 21, 23; 3:14, 17, 18; 4:1 (twice), 15, 19; 5:10. The noun occurs in 1:11; 4:13; 5:1, 9.) It is noteworthy that whereas in Paul the theology of the cross dominates, 1 Peter does not concentrate on the cross (the term is absent), but on suffering.

The author addresses the situation of his audience in Asia Minor in this way:

Beloved, do not be surprised at the fiery ordeal that is taking place among you to test you, as though something strange were happening to you. But rejoice insofar as you are sharing Christ's sufferings, so that you may also be glad and shout for joy when his glory is revealed. If you are reviled for the name of Christ, you are blessed, because the Spirit of glory, which is the Spirit of God, is resting on you. But let none of you suffer as a murderer, a thief, a criminal, or even a mischief maker. Yet if any of you suffers as a Christian, do not consider it a disgrace, but glorify God because you bear this name (4:12-16).

The text underscores both the intensity and the scope of the suffering the readers experience. The author compares Christian suffering with punishment as severe as that for murder, thievery, and criminal conduct. Moreover, its scope is worldwide: "You know that your brothers and sisters in all the world are undergoing the same kinds of suffering" (5:9). These Christians of Asia Minor are called "the exiles of the Dispersion" (1:1), and "aliens and exiles" (2:11). Their situation is clearly disclosed: They suffer the lot of outcasts and displaced persons in the very towns and cities where they live. As undesirable "aliens" (2:11), they are not only victims of social ostracism, but they also lack legal status and security in the socioeconomic and political context of the Roman Empire.

Although it is possible that the letter reflects the imminent persecution under the emperor Domitian (81–96 A.D.), it is more likely that the suffering of Christians is due to a hostile social system, which denounces Christians as "the hatred of the human race" (Tacitus). It is a situation of homelessness in the very place one calls one's native home and it is instigated by people of one's own socioeconomic class.

Thus 1 Peter does not portray a climactic and traumatic moment of acute suffering, but rather a suffering of a constant and persistent sort that wears people down because of its ceaseless, daily pressure. And yet the marginality and insecurity of these Christians in Asia Minor is somehow a reason for joy: "Although you have not seen him, you love him (Jesus Christ); and even though you do not see him now, you believe in him and rejoice with an indescribable and glorious joy, for you are receiving the outcome of your faith, the salvation of your souls" (1:8-9). Joy amidst suffering is possible, because the life and thought of these Christians is anchored in a twofold reality: that of their baptism (i.e., of "a new birth into a living hope through the resurrection of Jesus Christ from the dead" [1:3]), and that of a sure hope (i.e., of "having an inheritance . . . ready to be revealed in the last time" [1:4-5]).

These realities express themselves in a tightly knit support group—the housechurch—that gives social and spiritual cohesion to the lives of these Christians and enables them to devise strategies of hope amidst suffering. They know the power of the Spirit to be present among them, and the Spirit functions for them not only as the foretaste of God's final glory and kingdom (4:13; cf. 4:7), but also as the power that enables them to imitate Christ in the present (1:2; 2:21-25). And so the housechurches rejoice in the midst of suffering: "If you are reviled for the name of Christ, you are blessed, because the spirit of glory, which is the Spirit of God, is resting on you" (4:14). Indeed, joy in the midst of suffering is possible because it is the prelude to the joy at the coming of God's glory.

In the light of this hope, suffering can be both endured and realistically assessed. There is no need to repress it or to elevate it "spiritually."

Thus we notice that there is in 1 Peter a triadic bond between suffering, hope in the imminent manifestation of the kingdom of God, and the moral life. The letter emphasizes repeatedly the need for "good works" (2:12), "doing good" (2:15; cf. 3:13), and "good conduct" (2:12; 3:16). The author suggests that even if husbands do not obey the word, "they may be won over without a word by their wives' conduct (*anastrophē*) when they see the purity and reverence of your lives" (3:1-2).

Suffering, then, is made tolerable and even a matter for joy, because it is not the final destiny for these Christians, but is rather a penultimate reality: "Rejoice insofar as you are sharing Christ's sufferings, so that you may also be glad and shout for joy when his glory is revealed" (4:13). The triadic bond between suffering, the kingdom of God, and the moral life gives rise to a bifocal hope. The author believes that the hope in God's coming kingdom stimulates as well hopeful "missionary" possibilities for Christian faith in the midst of oppression.

Christian faith and life can show its attractiveness to outsiders and gain their respect, if not to make converts out of them. Thus Christian hope in 1 Peter has, in a sense, windows open to the world. Its interpretation of suffering in the world is not purely passive, but has redemptive and "hopeful" features. And so the author appeals to the "aliens" and "exiles": "Conduct yourselves honorably among the Gentiles, so that, though they malign you as evildoers, they may see your honorable deeds and glorify God when he comes to judge" (2:12). And again: "In your hearts sanctify Christ as Lord. Always be ready to make your defense (*apologia*) to anyone who demands from you an accounting for the hope that is in you; yet do it with gentleness and reverence. Keep your conscience clear, so that, when you are maligned, those who abuse you for your good conduct in Christ may be put to shame" (3:15-16).

Reflections on Suffering and Hope in 1 Peter

1 PETER DEMONSTRATES THAT OUR ASSESSMENTS OF SUFFERING and hope are closely related to our specific sociocultural location in the world. Social circumstances determine to a large extent how we cope with suffering and what we hope for. For instance, when we have reason to believe that the scope of suffering is a limited or passing phase, we

experience it with less intensity than when we know it to be a permanent reality.

The crucial concern in all this is, however, whether we succeed or fail in *relating* suffering and hope to each other. For when we dissociate suffering from hope, we either adopt a disposition of resignation and/or despair, or commit ourselves to trivial pursuits of hope. Thus our success or failure in relating suffering and hope will decide whether our suffering is going to be meaningful or meaningless, and whether our hope will be authentic or false.

In this respect, 1 Peter not only relates suffering to hope, but also shows how the scope and intensity of suffering matches the scope and intensity of hope (4:13; 5:8-10). For we recognize that a minimal presence or even total absence of suffering frequently produces only a "minimal" hope both in scope and intensity. When I hope exclusively for my individual well-being, whether on earth or in heaven, the scope of my hope is narrow, private, and exclusive, although, to be sure, its intensity may vary. But when my hope is focused on the restoration of the totality of God's created world and on the well-being of all its constituents, the scope of my hope is universal, communal, and inclusive. In this case, my hope will be intensive as well, because it cannot but yearn for the cessation of suffering, evil, and death in the world. And so we can say that when my suffering has a limited scope and/or duration, I will experience it less intensely than when its scope is extensive.

The question now arises whether 1 Peter is sufficiently helpful in answering the human dimensions of suffering in our world. Notwithstanding the danger of an anachronistic reading of a first-century document such as 1 Peter, some critical questions must be raised about its dealing with suffering. Although we can understand the manner in which the triadic field of suffering, ethics, and the kingdom of God functioned for the readers of 1 Peter, how shall we appropriate it today? Can 1 Peter become a catalytic text for us? (See my introduction, above.)

Is it possible to address human suffering adequately if we do not make important distinctions between several modes of suffering? It seems imperative to distinguish between suffering at the hands of human injustice and suffering at the hands of nature—that is, between suffering due to the power of human injustice and suffering due to the power of death. For that distinction points to the difference between meaningful and meaningless or tragic suffering. For instance, the death of Martin Luther King must be evaluated differently from the death of a person who, in his/her fullness of life, is suddenly stricken with cancer, or one who suffers the lot of a chronically, mentally ill person. We must make distinctions between these modes of suffering, because our ethical response to suffering must be congruent with its distinctive modes. Thus, our ethical response to suffering caused by human injustice and idolatry must be aggressive—it invites individual and communal strategies of overcoming, or at least limiting, the domain of that form of suffering.

However, our ethical response to suffering due to the power of death is bound to be different. Here the ethical imagination cannot find aggressive ways to counter this enemy. This mode of suffering is so unbearable, because it compels us to face the specter of meaningless and "hopeless" suffering. The curse of this form of suffering is its numbing and isolating power. It leaves us speechless, unable to express our affliction; it creates the loneliness of suffering and breaks the bond of human solidarity.

Whereas in New Testament terms we can say that the first mode of suffering—that caused by human injustice—invites redemptive or sacrifical suffering, the second mode of suffering—that caused by the power of death—causes New Testament authors to appeal to endurance and "patience" in view of the horizon of hope (i.e., the coming kingdom of God that will make all suffering cease).

It is clear that 1 Peter does not make the distinction between the several modes of suffering that are so crucial for our human inquiry into the meaning of suffering. Because the author emphasizes the apocalyptic dimension of hope in God's imminent glory and entertains "hopeful" strategies for mission, we expect to find in the letter an aggressive stance toward the injustice its readers suffer in society. However, 1 Peter counsels passive endurance and thus introduces a certain masochism into the church's mandate of redemptive suffering for the sake of its mission in the world. The author claims that unjust suffering is not something that Christians should avoid or protest; rather, it possesses an inherent virtue and carries a reward: "For it is a credit to you if, being aware of God, you endure pain while suffering unjustly. If you endure when you are beaten for doing wrong, what credit is that? But if you endure when you do right and suffer for it, you have God's approval" (2:19-20).

Moreover, the virtue of "good works" is in 1 Peter the consequence of a submissive piety, especially when the author urges Christians to adopt and submit to the moral and political dictates of the customs of Roman society (see the household codes of 2:18—3:7 and the mandate to submit to civil authorities in 2:13-17).

Thus, since the author does not envisage the issue of suffering due to the power of death in this world, he locates the virtue of endurance in the

wrong place. For if the ethical response to the power of injustice is reduced to passive endurance, Christians are compelled to view unjust suffering as a form of grace (3:20) and testing (4:12), as if God's grace
encourages masochism!

Moreover, how adequate is the author's conception of Christ as our
example? The author says: "Christ also suffered for you, leaving you an
example, so that you should follow in his steps. . . . When he was
abused, he did not return abuse; when he suffered, he did not threaten;
but he entrusted himself to the one who judges justly. He himself bore
our sins in the body on the cross . . ." (2:21, 23-24).

At this point the question arises how can the author make a direct
connection between the redemptive suffering of Christ for "our sins"
(2:24) and the unjust suffering of Christians because of human oppression? And this raises a more general question: Is it really adequate to
apply the redemptive suffering of Christ to every kind of suffering
people experience? Since the suffering of Christ had a meaningful
purpose—to inaugurate God's kingdom among us—we must be very
careful lest we apply without more ado his meaningful suffering to the
various forms of meaningless suffering in our world.

CHAPTER 15

The Book of Revelation

Basic Structure

A. Preface, 1:1-3

B. Letter Opening, 1:4-8

C. Part I—Prophetical Call and Vision, 1:9-20, 1:19: Theme of Book: "Now write what you have *seen* (1:9-20), *what is* (chapters 2 and 3), and what is to take place *after this* (chapters 4–22)

D. Part II—The Letters to the Seven Churches, 2:1—3:22

E. Part III—4:1—22:5

    1. Introduction, 4:1—5:14: The Theophany (chapter 4); the Lamb and the Book with the Seven Seals (chapter 5)

    2. The Seven Seals, 6:1—8:1

    3. The Seven Trumpets, 8:2—11:19

    4. Core of the Book: The Battle of the Evil Powers, 12:1—14:20

    5. The Seven Bowls, 15:1—16:21

    6. The Fall of Babylon, 17:1—19:10

    7. Destruction of the Hostile Powers, 19:11—20:15

    8. The New World, 21:1—22:5

F. Conclusion; Comments, 22:6-21

The phrase *"after this"* (*meta tauta*; 1:19c) reinforces 1:1, "The revelation of Jesus Christ, which God gave him to show his servants *what must soon take place*" (*en tachei*), and also 1:3b, "for the time is *near*" (*engys*). The sense of the imminent end pervades the book: 2:16; 3:11; 11:14; 12:12; 22:6, 7, 10, 12, 20 (cf. also the frequent references to phrases such as "no more delay" (10:6); "a little longer" (6:11; 20:3; with respect to the devil: "his time is short" [12:12]). Notice as well the sense of an ending in

125

10:7, "in the days when the seventh angel is to blow his trumpet, the mystery of God will be fulfilled," and in 16:17, "It is done" (*gegonen*; cf. also 11:7; 15:1, 8; 17:17; 20:3, 5, 7).

The narrative is regularly interrupted by hymns which anticipate the final victory of God (7:9-16; 11:15-19; 12:10-12; 15:1-8, and 19:1-9). The interlude of 10:1 — 11:14, which interrupts the sequence between the sixth and seventh trumpet (9:13; 12:15) functions to contemporize for the church the cosmic events, described in the vision of the seven trumpets.

The author, John, presents himself as a prophet (*doulos*) and his book as a word of prophecy (*logos tēs prophēteias*; 1:3; 20:7, 10, 18). While he refers to it as "a book" (*biblion*) or as "the words of the prophecy of this book" (*tous logous tēs prophēteias tou bibliou toutou*; 1:11; 22:7, 10, 18-19), he ascribes to it absolute canonical authority (22:18-19). It should be noticed that the author mentions "the gospel" only once (14:6: the angel with "the eternal gospel"), which, however, has no specific Christian content, since it represents a call to repentence in face of God's imminent judgment.

The Book of Revelation and the Nature of Apocalyptic Theology

THE REVELATION OF JOHN (= *REVELATION*) OCCUPIES AN UNFORTU-nate place in the canon of Scripture. Because Genesis is the first book in the Bible and Revelation the last, it may suggest that the Bible moves from a supernatural beginning (God's creation of the world) to its super-natural ending and closure (Revelation). Just as creation had a far-away beginning, so it has a far-off ending. In fact, the position of Revelation at the very end of the canon has distorted its importance in at least two ways:

First, it became for orthodox Christianity an almost irrelevant ap-pendix. Because Christ was conceived as the eschatological center of his-tory and thus as the exclusive criterion of salvation, the end of history had already appeared in him so that attention to the end of the world can only mean illegitimate speculation. Bultmann, for instance, states that since the Christ-event, history has been swallowed up by eschatology. One may even wonder whether the genre of apocalyptic literature has a legitimate place in Christian thought. For, if our salvation is anchored in the Christ-event, an apocalyptic scenario, consisting of predictions and anxious speculations about the end of the world, belie the blessings we have already been given in Christ.

Along these lines, Revelation has been suspect in Christian theology from the beginning. The *Alogi* (second century) attributed both the Gospel and the Revelation of John to the archheretic Cerinthus. Bishop Dionysius of Alexandria (third century) rejected Revelation because it was not written by the apostle John. Later on, Calvin omitted to write a commentary on Revelation, although he provided commentaries on all other books of the Bible, and Luther cherished a very dim view of the book and questioned its authenticity.

In this context we must notice that the interpretation of apocalyptic has been largely a stream of misinterpretation in the history of the church. From J. Wellhausen and B. Duhm until recent times, apocalyptic has been villified as armchair sophistry, degeneration of prophecy, utopian speculation, ethical passivity, and so on (cf. A. Jülicher, "Apocalyptic is prophecy turned into baroque").

Christian theologians disdain the use of the term "apocalyptic" because it is considered to be a pejorative term that pertains to weird speculations and visionary experiences. "Eschatology," to the contrary, is deemed to be a safe term. In fact, "eschatology" in neo-orthodox circles becomes a term that no longer has any precise meaning. Usually it defines the Christ-event as God's ultimate revelatory word. Paul Althaus's statement is typical in this respect: "The world has in principle its end in the judgment and the kingdom in Christ. In this sense every time in history and likewise history as a whole, is an end-time, because both individually and as a whole it borders upon eternity and has an immediate relation to its judgment and its redemption. *To this extent all the hours of history are the self-same last hour.*"[1]

Second, the position of Revelation at the end of the biblical canon distorted its importance in another, yet related way. It encouraged heretical speculations and discouraged a historical interpretation of the book. It became the pretext for contemporary interpretations, and its mysterious symbols were applied to diverse historical figures, such as the Papacy, Napoleon, Hitler, and more recently, to post–World War II events.[2]

---

[1]Paul Althaus, *Die letzten Dinge* (7th ed.; Gütersloh: C. Bertelsmann, 1957) 272 (my emphasis and translation).
[2]Cf. Hal Lindsey, *The Late Great Planet Earth* (Grand Rapids, Mich.: Zondervan, 1970).

In order to appreciate the intent of Revelation, it is necessary to make a distinction between apocalyptic theology and the literary genre of apocalyptic or, more precisely, we must distinguish apocalyptic as a literary genre, a sociological movement, and as a series of theological motifs.[3]

"Apocalypse" means an unveiling in a visionary manner of what pertains to the end of history. In short, it refers basically to the coming glory and triumph of God over the evil powers that oppose him. Thus in Luke's Gospel Simeon praises God when he sees Jesus in the temple: "My eyes have seen your salvation, which you have prepared in the presence of all peoples, a light for revelation (*apokalypsis*) to the Gentiles and for glory (*doxa*) to your people Israel" (Luke 2:30-32). Likewise, Paul looks forward to the final "*apokalypsis*" of God: "For the creation waits with eager longing for the revealing of the children of God" (Rom. 8:19). In the New Testament, "revelation" has most frequently a saving aspect (Rom. 1:17), something in which to rejoice (1 Pet. 5:1), and to be ardently expected (Rom. 8:18-30), because its saving character has been anticipated in God's revelation in Jesus Christ (Rom. 1:17; Gal. 1:16). Accordingly, the author of Revelation opens his book by announcing "the revelation of Jesus Christ, which God gave him" (1:1). Within the daily practice of the churches, *apokalypsis* is synonymous with prophecy and with comfort/exhortation (*paraklēsis*; 1 Cor. 14:6, 26). It is a prophecy about God's final glory and as well an exhortation that gives comfort to believers. Consequently, it is also a call to endurance and perseverance amidst suffering and persecution (Rev. 13:10; 14:12). Thus Revelation — the book of *apokalypsis* (1:1) — calls itself a "word of prophecy" (1:3; 22:7, 10, 18) and addresses the churches in this manner (2:7, 11, 16; 3:20).

Although Christian apocalyptic theology shares many features with Jewish apocalyptic thought, its distinctive emphases can be listed as follows:

1. A *dualism* between this age of Satan and his allies, and the coming age of God's glorious triumph. This apocalyptic dualism is born out of a fundamental contradiction between legitimate expectations based on God's promises to his people and their empirical reality.

2. An ardent expectation of the *imminent coming* of God's triumph over the powers of sin and death which rule the world. Apocalyptic theology is not engaged in a philosophical teleology or in a speculative

---

[3]Cf. Paul Hanson, "Apocalyptic Literarture," *The Hebrew Bible and Its Modern Interpreters*, ed. D. A. Knight & G. M. Tucker (Chico, Calif.: Scholars Press, 1985) 465–88.

periodization of world history. Rather, it expects the imminent actualization of God's promises, especially because they have been ratified and intensified since Christ's death and resurrection.

3. A *determinism* that posits the inevitable outcome of God's plan of salvation. For instance, the book with the seven seals in Revelation 5 shows that with the opening of the seals the historical process is completely determined by God's fixed plan. Accordingly, the apocalyptic term "must" (*dei*) pervades the book (1:1; 4:11; 10:11; 11:5; 13:10; 17:10; 20:3; 22:6; cf., for example, the phrase, "what must soon take place" [1:1; 22:6]).

4. The *universal scope* of God's triumph, it involves the redemption of the whole created order and thus the defeat of death as the last enemy ("Then Death and Hades were thrown into the lake of fire" [20:14]). God's universal triumph thus transcends ethnic (Jewish) privileges and the particularity of "in-groups."

5. The hope in God's imminent triumph that enables believers to endure amidst suffering and persecution is anchored in *God's faithfulness* to his promises, as revealed in Christ (see 2 above). Language of God's and Christ's trustworthiness abounds in Revelation: "Jesus Christ the faithful (*pistos*) witness" (1:5); "The words of the Amen (*ho Amēn*), the faithful (*pistos*) and true (*alēthinos*) witness, the origin of God's creation" (3:14); "Then I saw heaven opened, and there was a white horse! Its rider is called Faithful (*pistos*) and True . . ." (19:11); "And they sing the song of Moses, the Servant of God, and the song of the Lamb: 'Great and amazing are your deeds, Lord God the Almighty! just (*dikaios*) and true (*alēthinos*) are your ways, King of the nations' " (15:3; cf. 16:7; 19:2).

We must be aware that apocalyptic theology is the crucial ingredient of every New Testament author. Rather than being reduced to a last item in the biblical canon, it pervades all of New Testament thought. And even when some New Testament authors do not espouse the futuristic element of apocalyptic theology, they have to come to terms with it by strategies of modifications (cf., e.g., Matthew; Luke-Acts) or of suppression (cf., e.g., Colossians; Ephesians).

Apocalyptic theology attempts to answer the question of theodicy in the face of existential suffering. It refuses to explain suffering solely as God's punishment or as his pedagogy and testing. Moreover, it refuses to find comfort in the prudence or skepticism of a theology of wisdom (cf., for example, Heb. 12:5-11) or by appealing to the mysterious transcendence of a God who will not answer (Job). Moreover, it refuses to surrender hope in the redemption of God's creation by retreating into an otherworldly individualism.

Thus Christian apocalyptic theology becomes distorted when, in view of the experience of hopelessness and of evil in this world, it substitutes an otherworldly "in-group" utopia for the transformation of God's total creation. Genuine apocalyptic theology, then, is not an "opium" for the oppressed of this world!

How Christian Is the Book of Revelation?

NOTWITHSTANDING THE FACT THAT REVELATION SHARES MANY features with an authentic Christian apocalyptic theology (see above), it also transgresses some of the crucial mandates of such a theology. It eclipses the universal scope of hope in favor of a particularism that celebrates an elitist in-group and dismisses hope in the transformation of God's whole creation. Thus Revelation limits salvation to the 144,000 who have been redeemed from the earth (14:1-5). Moreover, "Only those who are written in the Lamb's book of life" (21:27) are worthy to enter "the holy city Jerusalem coming down out of heaven from God" (21:10). In fact, this sectarian disposition carries within it the danger of an absolute dualism between church and world, so that the world of God's creation is, as it were, removed from God's rule and surrendered to Satan. Indeed, suffering in Revelation has become so absolute that it leads inevitably to death and martyrdom, and hope is so antithetical to the realm of suffering that it becomes a purely otherworldly hope. Although the scope of hope is universal in Revelation (cf. the expectation of a new heaven and a new earth (21:1-5), and although it awaits the imminent and complete transvaluation of all present worldly values, it sees—unlike 1 Peter—no possibilities of redemptive action in and for the world. In this situation hope becomes infested not only with utopian, otherworldly features, but also with a disposition of hostility and a desire for revenge toward the enemy: "Come, gather for the great supper of God, to eat the flesh of kings, the flesh of captains, the flesh of mighty, the flesh of horses and their riders—flesh of all, both free and slave, both small and great" (19:17-18; cf. also 21:8; 22:12).

What is even more crucial is the question whether the genre of an apocalyptic *narrative* can do justice to the character of a genuine Christian apocalyptic theology. For how can a sequential and chronological narrative—that is, an apocalyptic program—do justice to the expectation of the one ultimate closure event—the triumph of God that alone should occupy Christian hope? Do we not have to say that—after the initiation of the kingdom of God in the death and resurrection of Christ—Christian hope should be exclusively fixed on God's public confirmation of his provisional act in Christ? Is it not true that the present time is the only penultimate time before the end time of God's theophany? However, Revelation's narrative sketches a sequence of events to come, reinforced by continuous references to "what is to take place hereafter" (1:19; 4:1-2; 7:1, 9; 9:12; 15:5; 18:1; 19:1; 20:3). These references serve to connect the various successive scenes in order to bring the narrative to its final closure.

This history-like sketch of events-to-come makes Revelation liable to predictions and speculations—that is, it can be argued that an apocalyptic *narrative* is a secondary form of genuine Christian apocalyptic theology. It programs events to come and thus causes a postponement of the imminence of God's final triumph. In this manner it intends to come to terms with an ongoing history and with the delay of the Parousia—that is, with an ongoing history, if not with a disappointed hope.

Notwithstanding these critical observations about Revelation as a historical narrative of events that must precede the final triumph of God, some scholars have suggested that a different perspective on this issue may help us to understand the true intent of the author of Revelation.

From this perspective the historical narrative with its successive scenes has a symbolic function—it is meant to produce a heightened tension and a call to endurance (chapters 2 and 3; 13:10; 14:12). Thus, when the reader is convinced, "Now the end is here," the series of the seven seals, the seven trumpets, and the seven bowls serve to accentuate the dramatic tension for the reader. For the series of sevens dovetail in a parallel fashion to heighten the tension, although it seems that one series alone suffices to score the desired point. Moreover, the tension in the narrative is further heightened by the frequent preludes and interludes of hymnic confessions that celebrate the "already" of Christ's victory in heaven—a victory anticipated as well by the core of the book (chapters 12–14). Since these chapters intend to concretize the symbolic descriptions of the cosmic battle depicted in the series of the seven trumpets, passages such as 10:7 have a similar symbolic function: The text announces the final end when the seventh trumpet will be sounded with the words, "No more delay," although the seventh trumpet actually does not sound until 11:15 while it is subsequently succeeded by other sequences of symbolic images, until finally the end is actualized in chapter 21.

From this symbolic perspective, the true meaning of the apocalyptic narrative consists of two basic themes: one, the exhortation to endure in the knowledge that Christ has already defeated Satan and his minions in heaven; and two, the ability to discern what gives us true life in contrast to the false promises of life that the world's powers promise us. Hence, the frequent contrasting parallelism in Revelation between the Lamb and the Beast: both have mortal wounds (5:6, 9, 12; 13:2-13); those who follow the Beast and those who follow the Lamb both carry marks on their foreheads (7:3; 13:6-17; 14:1-5, 9–11).

Conclusion

THE BASIC QUESTION, THEN, THAT THE INTERPRETATION OF REVelation poses does not permit an easy answer. I phrase it this way: To what extent is an apocalyptic narrative — that is, an apocalyptic program — however much intended to instill hope in the immediate fulfillment of God's final triumph — an unsuitable vehicle for an authentic Christian apocalyptic theology? For such a narrative suggests that we presently do not actually live in the end time — in the interim between the Christ-event and the kingdom of God — but rather in a plurality of penultimate times, which give birth to a series of future events to come *before* God's kingdom can be actualized.

Since Revelation deflates *our* time as the end time and points to other times to come as preliminary to the end time, it runs counter to a genuine Christian apocalyptic theology, such as we find in Paul's end time hope (cf. 1 Thess. 4:15; 5:1-11; Rom. 8:18-19; 1 Cor. 15:51). And so my question remains: Does a symbolic reading of Revelation help us or hinder us in strengthening our profound yearning for God's final triumph over the evil and suffering that rule our world?

CHAPTER 16

Unity and Diversity in the New Testament

AFTER MY DISCUSSION OF THE MOST IMPORTANT BOOKS OF THE New Testament, the reader must wonder if any unity can be found among the multifarious voices in the New Testament. For if the New Testament is to have normative authority for us, so that all Christian life and thought must conform to the norm of the New Testament, it seems that these chapters—concentrating on the diversity of the New Testament writings—destroy every possible trace of its unity. Indeed, can we claim that the so-different voices of the New Testament authors constitute a coherent-authoritative unity rather than a chaotic multiplicity?

As we have seen, even the seemingly consistent perspective within some New Testament books, for example, the Letters of Paul, betray an amazing variety of perspectives. And this variety is even more astute when we consider the writings of Paul's pupils (Ephesians and the Pastoral Epistles). And when we move from the Letters of Paul and his pupils to books such as 1 Peter, Hebrews, and Revelation, we find ourselves in very different worlds of thought. Moreover, the reader will ask how the great variety within the Gospels can produce a unified perspective apart from the even more troublesome question whether the various gospel accounts can be harmonized with the diverse epistolary sections of the New Testament.

Indeed, when we speak about the authority of Scripture in our time, we are engaged, it seems, in an anachronistic exercise. What meaning does the term "biblical authority" have other than being an inherent, routinized concept that comes to us from the tradition as some holy entity? In what sense, then, is it anything but a piece of tradition, which is nothing but a relic from the past that has ceased to have any existential meaning for us?

In fact, if we desire to speak at all about the authority of Scripture, it seems that we are able to speak only about its *incidental* rather than its *normative authority*. However, a moment's reflection must convince us that an incidental authority constitutes an outright logical contradiction, because the notion of authority is necessarily linked with its normative and abiding character. As soon as authority is qualified as incidental, it ceases to be authority in any intelligible sense. For an incidental authority is an ad hoc, subjective estimate of what may be only fitting in a very particular and contingent situation.

Of course, this observation should not come as a surprise to us. Our time is characterized by an almost total eclipse of authoritative structures in our culture. When we reflect on the road we have traveled since the Reformation, it becomes abundantly evident how unclear, uncertain, and ambivalent we have become about the authority of Scripture, the written word of God, which we confess to be the normative source of Christian life and doctrine. The 1967 Confession of the Presbyterian Church (USA) claims that "Scripture is the word of God written." This formulation (actually, it is more akin to post-Reformation orthodoxy than to either Luther or Calvin with its insistence on the written character of the canon of Scripture) posits a severe challenge to us. Can we in our time simply regress to the tradition of the sixteenth century in our view of Scripture?

Since the Enlightenment the answer to this question has been a resounding "No!" Indeed, the eclipse of the Reformation's insistence on the normative and critical function of the New Testament has been due to the Enlightenment; it produced a new sense of human autonomy and of historical consciousness. New criteria of historical explanation were posited, climaxing in E. Troeltsch's widely accepted theory that critical-historical inquiry rests on three interrelated principles: (1) *the principle of criticism*, which focuses on the critical distance of the observer from the historical text and on the fact that judgments of the past can only attain a greater or lesser degree of probability and are always open to revision; (2) *the principle of analogy*, or internal relations; and (3) *the principle of correlation*, which stresses the historical nexus between phenomena. Thus, since the Enlightenment, the principle of the authority of Scripture broke down. The discovery of the historical origins of the diverse books of the canon led to a view of Scripture as a bundle of various time-bound, culturally specific documents subject to the canons of historical inquiry.

We must realize that this view of Scripture is the dominant one today. A visit to any recent conference of the guild of biblical scholars will demonstrate the extent to which we have cast aside the issue of normative biblical authority. Indeed, we have substituted the notion of the Bible as an archaeological-historical deposit for one of the Bible as an authoritative *viva vox* (living voice) for the community of faith. And thus the authority of the Bible is among us at best an incidental authority, becoming authoritative when and if it conforms in some of its expressions to what we consider to be helpful guidelines for our present situation.

In opposition to the prevailing scholarly climate which, in its commitment to the principles of the Enlightenment, proposes that the conception of a "New Testament theology" must be displaced by a "history of early Christian religion,"[1] I intend to reclaim the normative authority of the New Testament. For we must realize that the question of the *authority* of the New Testament is intimately connected to the issue of its *unity*. Therefore, the problem of the unity of the New Testament amidst its variety is a crucial issue for Christians today. If that issue is bypassed in favor of a historicist view of the New Testament, the claim of the New Testament on us is brought to naught and replaced by a voyeurism of detached observation that dissects the New Testament according to its own interests and has no interest in the unity of the New Testament.

Before addressing the problem of the unity and diversity of the New Testament and thus of its normative authority, I must discuss an issue that is directly related to it: the significance of the canon of the New Testament for Christian life and thought. It is a crucial mistake of recent New Testament scholarship to simply dismiss the notion of canonicity in its probing of the various New Testament documents.

Räisänen applauds Wrede's comments on this issue: "Anyone who treats these writings [of the New Testament] as such [i.e., canonical] in historical work places himself under the authorities of the bishops and theologians of the second to fourth centuries."[2] However, he forgets—in the company of many other scholars—that the New Testament is primarily a book of the church. After all, what intrinsic importance does the New Testament possess when we isolate it from its foundational place in and for the church? The various books of the New Testament hardly

---

[1]Cf. W. Wrede and Räisänen in Heikki Räisänen, *Beyond New Testament Theology* (London and Philadelphia: SCM and Trinity Press International, 1990) 16.
[2]Ibid, p.13.

deserve the epithet "classic," when we divorce them from their impact on church and culture (*Wirkungsgeschichte*). Indeed, apart from its canonical significance, the New Testament would probably draw not much more attention than a letter of Seneca or a treatise of Lucretius.

Moreover, the New Testament is the book of the church in another respect. Luther recognized that the church must conform its life and thought to the criterion of Scripture when he posited Scripture not only as the norm, but also as the critical voice for ecclesiastical doctrine. This criterion that insists that the church is to be obedient to the voices of the *whole* canon has two important implications: first, we cannot posit a "canon within the canon." For, although it is an empirical fact that most of us operate with such a "canon within the canon" because certain sections of the New Testament appeal to us more directly than others, we must realize not only that different segments of the New Testament canon speak to us in different moments and situations of our life, but also that the church catholic has drawn nourishment from the whole canon throughout its long life.

Second, the canonical significance of the New Testament in the life of the church dictates that the so-called extracanonical books—even those contemporaneous with some canonical New Testament writings—cannot claim an equal place of authority with the canonical New Testament books. Notwithstanding the intrinsic religious and historical importance of the extracanonical writings, the decision by the church over the centuries to exclude them from the canon should not be reversed. Therefore, I reject the position of many New Testament historians and theologians who espouse a so-called "open canon."[3] For once the boundaries of the canon are wiped out, the issue of what constitutes the norm of Scripture is washed away while the sufficiency of the present New Testament canon for the life of the church is disregarded.

So how do we account for the unity and diversity of the New Testament? We confess the writings of the New Testament to convey the power of the gospel ever anew to different times and circumstances. Thus we must reject the notion of the New Testament as a purely historical and archaeological deposit. However, how can we posit the normative authority of the New Testament in the face of its historically dated

[3]See for instance E. Stauffer, *New Testament Theology* (New York: Macmillan, 1955) and H. Koester, "The Intentions and Scope of Trajectories," *Trajectories through Early Christianity*, ed. J. M. Robinson & H. Koester (Philadelphia: Fortress Press, 1971) 269–79.

and culturally specific features that determine, to a large extent, its great diversity? Indeed, a return to the tradition of the sixteenth century with respect to the unity of the New Testament is no longer possible (see above). Luther's view of the harmonious unity of Scripture is no longer a viable option for us; it is simply not true that the diversity of the New Testament is at one with its essential unity. Moreover, recent attempts to harmonize the various New Testament authors with each other, or to save the unity of the New Testament by neglecting the particularity of the different books by means of a dogmatic, topical approach, must be rejected.

The solution that I proposed with respect to the unity of Paul's gospel amidst the great variety of emphases in his letters (see above) seems also applicable to the greater compass of the New Testament as a whole. Therefore, I want to introduce a twofold model that may assist us in clarifying the problem of the authority of the New Testament and to reassert its basic unity for our time.

The first part of the model posits that the New Testament is constituted by two components: coherence and contingency (see above, the introduction). Moreover, these two components are interrelated in a complex manner. I define coherence as the abiding, constant, and normative elements of the gospel, which focus on the apocalyptic–eschatological interpretation of the life, death, and resurrection of Christ. Contingency, on the other hand, concerns those elements of Scripture that comprise the time-bound, culturally specific situations into and for which the gospel is addressed. Furthermore, we must recognize that the interaction between coherence and contingency constitutes the heart of the gospel; it makes the abiding Word of God a word on target for the people to whom the gospel is proclaimed. This is so because it is the very essence of the gospel that it asserts itself into the particularities of every human situation.

Indeed, once we divorce the coherence of the gospel from its contingency, we are no longer dealing with the gospel but, rather, with some eternal verity, a pronouncement that resembles more a universally valid, philosophical proposition than it does the particularity of the gospel. In this case, the Word of the gospel disintegrates into a monotonous monologue, similar to the description by Vincens of Lerins in the fifth century about true doctrine in the Catholic Church, "that which has been believed everywhere, always and by all" (*ubique . . . semper . . . ab omnibus*). However, if we divorce the contingency of the gospel from its necessary interaction with the coherent core, the gospel disintegrates into an incidental and opportunistic structure. It now accommodates itself to what-ever the fashions of the time demand and into what the marketplace is willing to buy, or worse still, it becomes prey for whatever ideological position happens to rule our time.

Thus, when we posit that the authority of Scripture is to be located in the dynamic interrelation between coherence and contingency, the question of the authority and unity of the New Testament is directly re-lated to the interpretation of the New Testament. It follows that the New Testament is only authoritative when we obey its command to engage in the same risks of interpreting the gospel in which it is itself engaged in all its parts. And so we can say that the authority of the New Testament is identical with its incarnational effectiveness in the human situation, an effectiveness that pertains both to its critical, judgmental function—its over-againstness—and to its transforming, liberating function. In other words, the essence of the authority of the New Testament lies in its two-fold dimension: its incarnational dimension (its concrete insertion into the particularity of human situations) and its transcendent dimension (its critical over-againstness with respect to human pride, idolatry, and the autonomy of the ego).

The second part of the twofold model concerns the issue of the trans-fer of the gospel to our time. However, we must be aware that the inter-pretive task of conjoining coherence and contingency is directly related to the issue of the transfer of the gospel from biblical times to our time. Indeed, the Word of the New Testament can only be a lively word, a word on target, when we realize that its central message must speak to us within the particularity of our diverse situations—in the same manner it functioned originally.

Therefore, I suggest that the authority of the New Testament has a catalytic function for our time. A catalytic reading of the New Testament denotes a generative hermeneutic. It means that even though the biblical text must undergo a necessary change in its transferral to our time, it is nonetheless not altered in its "substance." A catalytic hermeneutic in-tends to remain faithful to the abiding and normative coherence of the gospel, but in such a way that it resists a literalistic and anachronistic transfer of the text because it is aware that the contingent situations of biblical times are not identical to those of our time. For instance, the cul-turally conditioned New Testament voices about submission of slaves to masters and of women to men, and the New Testament's prevalent an-drocentrism simply cannot claim to be authoritative for us. In short, a catalytic view of a text's authority must follow the model of the authors of the New Testament in so interpreting the gospel that its claim on our time is neither anachronistic (as in a literalist hermeneutic), nor modernistic (as when the text simply becomes a means for confirming our own ideologies and prior convictions).

In what sense, then, is the twofold model that I outlined helpful in clarifying the unity/diversity problem in the New Testament? We must realize that the New Testament is not an infallible, inerrant book, but rather a collection of various commentaries on the abiding core of the gospel. The coherent framework of the New Testament—that is, its normative pattern for Christians—must be located in and derived from the gospel of God's saving purpose for the world, as manifested in the death and resurrection of Christ. In a similar way, Luther proposed as the norm and unified center of Scripture *"was Christum treibet."*

In short, the unity/diversity issue in the New Testament must be viewed as the attempt of the New Testament authors to interpret the core of the gospel in such a way that it becomes a word on target for the diverse contingent situations of the various audiences they address. And so we see these authors engaged in coherent strategies that must mediate the core of the gospel to the contingencies they face. In so doing, they—like we in our time—are forced to accept the risks that every imaginative interpreter of the gospel must face.

The diversity in the New Testament, then, invites us to engage in a critical reading of the New Testament, because we must continuously be alert to whether a text of the New Testament conforms to Luther's dictum *"was Christum treibet."* Indeed, the unity among the diversity of the New Testament must be located in the incarnational depth of the gospel that inserts itself into the wide variety of diverse human needs and problems. For we must be aware that *a unity without diversity* ascribes to the New Testament a monolithic, dogmatic homogeneity that simply imposes itself on the human situation and tends to elevate the contingencies of the New Testament into the coherent unity of the gospel. Similarly, *a diversity without unity* either accepts a "canon within the canon" in the New Testament to the exclusion of the other New Testament documents or simply dismisses from the New Testament what is not deemed to be relevant to the taste of the time.

Thus the authority of the New Testament for our time can only become a normative authority rather than an incidental authority, if we as interpreters of the New Testament will be able to discern the unified coherent pattern that pervades it in order to make it, with the help of the Holy Spirit, a living voice for our time.

BIBLIOGRAPHY

Althaus, Paul. *Die letzten Dinge.* 7th ed.; Gütersloh: C. Bertelsmann, 1957.

Barrett, C. K. *The Second Epistle to the Corinthians.* HNTC; New York: Harper & Row, 1973.

Barth, Karl. *The Resurrection of the Dead.* New York: Fleming H. Revell, 1933.

Bornkamm, Günther. "Die Vorgeschichte des sogennanten Zweiten Korintherbriefes." In *Gesammelte Aufsätze.* BEvT 53; Munich: C. Kaiser, 1971. 4.162–94.

Brox, N. "Amt, Kirche und Theologie in der nachapostolischen Epoche: Die Pastoralbriefe." In *Gestalt und Anspruch des Neuen Testaments.* Ed. J. Schreiner. Würzburg: Echter-Verlag, 1969. 120–33.

———. *Die Pastoralbriefe.* RNT 7:2; Regensburg: Verlag F. Pustet, 1969.

Bruce, F. F. *Paul: Apostle of the Heart Set Free.* Grand Rapids, Mich.: Eerdmans, 1977.

Cullmann, Oscar. *The Christology of the New Testament.* Trans. S. C. Guthrie and C. A. M. Hall. Rev. ed.; Philadelphia: Westminster Press, 1963.

Dibelius, Martin, and Hans Conzelmann. *The Pastoral Epistles.* Trans. P. Buttolph and A. Yarbro. Hermeneia; Philadelphia: Fortress Press, 1972.

Dodd, C. H. *The Meaning of Paul for Today.* New York: George H. Doran, 1920.

Donfried, Karl P. "False Presuppositions in the Study of Romans." In *The Romans Debate.* Minneapolis: Augsburg, 1977. 120–48.

Ebeling, Gerhard. *The Problem of Historicity in the Church and Its Proclamation.* Trans. G. Foley. Philadelphia: Fortress Press, 1967.

Fischer, K. M. "Anmerkungen zur Pseudepigraphie im Neuen Testament." *NTS* 23 (1977). 76–79.

Fitzmyer, Joseph A. *The Gospel according to Luke (I–IX).* AB; Garden City, N.Y.: Doubleday, 1981.

Funk, Robert W. *Language, Hermeneutic and Word of God: The Problem of Language in the New Testament and Contemporary Theology.* New York: Harper & Row, 1966.

Georgi, Dieter. *The Opponents of Paul in Second Corinthians.* Philadelphia: Fortress Press, 1986.

Hanson, Paul. "Apocalyptic Literarture." In *The Hebrew Bible and Its Modern Interpreters.* Ed. D. A. Knight and G. M. Tucker. Chico, Calif.: Scholars Press, 1985. 465–88.

Johnson, Luke T. *The Writings of the New Testament: An Interpretation.* Philadelphia: Fortress Press, 1986.

Kähler, Martin. *The So-called Historical Jesus and the Historic, Biblical Christ.* Trans. C. Braaten. Philadelphia: Fortress Press, 1964.

Käsemann, Ernst. *The Wandering People of God.* Trans. R. A. Harrisville and I. L. Sandberg. Minneapolis: Augsburg Press, 1984.

Kelber, Werner H. *Mark's Story of Jesus.* Philadelphia: Fortress Press, 1979.

Kierkegaard, S. *Philosophical Fragments.* Princeton, N.J.: Princeton University Press, 1962.

Koester, H. "The Intentions and Scope of Trajectories." In *Trajectories through Early Christianity.* Ed. J. M. Robinson and H. Koester. Philadelphia: Fortress Press, 1971. 269–79.

Kümmel, W. G. *Introduction to the New Testament.* Trans. H. C. Kee. Rev. ed. Nashville: Abingdon Press, 1975.

_____. *Das Neue Testament: Geschichte der Erforschung seiner Probleme.* Freiburg/ München: Verlag Karl Alber, 1958.

Lindsey, Hal. *The Late Great Planet Earth.* Grand Rapids, Mich.: Zondervan, 1970.

Lohse, Eduard. *The Formation of the New Testament.* Trans. M. E. Boring. Nashville: Abingdon, 1981.

MacDonald, D. R. *The Legend and the Apostle: The Battle for Paul in Story and Canon.* Philadelphia: Westminster, 1983.

Martin, Ralph P. *2 Corinthians.* WBC 40; Waco, Tex.: Word Books, 1985.

Marxsen, Willi. *Mark the Evangelist.* Trans. J. Boyce, et al. Nashville: Abingdon Press, 1969.

Matera, Frank J. *What Are They Saying about Mark?* New York: Paulist Press, 1987.

Mowry, L. "The Early Circulation of Paul's Letters." *JBL* 63 (1964) 73–86.

Pascal, Blaise. "Le Mystère de Jésus." In *Pensées sur la Religion et sur quelques autres sujets.* 2nd ed. Paris: Delmas, 1952.

Perrin, Norman. *The New Testament: An Introduction.* New York: Harcourt Brace Jovanovich, 1974.

Powell, Mark A. *What Are They Saying about Luke?* New York: Paulist Press, 1989.

Räisänen, Heikki. *Beyond New Testament Theology.* London: SCM and Philadelphia: Trinity Press International, 1990.

Robinson, James M. "Hermeneutic Since Barth." In *The New Hermeneutic.* Ed. J. M. Robinson & J. B. Cobb, Jr. NFT 2; New York: Harper & Row, 1964. 1–77.

Roloff, Jürgen. *Die Apostelgeschichte.* NTD 5; Göttingen: Vandenhoeck & Ruprecht, 1981.

Schelkle, K. H. *Das Neue Testament.* Kevelaer Rhineland: Butzon & Bercker, 1963.

Schmithals, W. "Die Korintherbriefe als Briefsammlung." *ZNW* 64 (1973) 263–88.

Schubert, Paul. *Form and Function of the Pauline Thanksgivings.* BZNW 20; Giessen/Berlin: Töpelmann, 1939.

Schweitzer, Albert. *The Quest of the Historical Jesus.* Intro. J. M. Robinson. New York: Macmillan, 1968.

Stauffer, E. *New Testament Theology.* New York: Macmillan, 1955.

Tannehill, Robert C. *The Narrative Unity of Luke-Acts: A Literary Interpretation.* Vol. 1. Philadelphia: Fortress Press, 1986.

Tillich, Paul. *Systematic Theology.* vol. 2. Chicago: University of Chicago Press, 1957.

Whitehead, Alfred N. *Religion in the Making.* New York: Macmillan, 1926.

Wrede, W. *The Messianic Secret.* London: James Clark, 1971.

Index of Modern Authors

Index of Biblical Passages

144

152